OXFORD PROGRESSIVE ENGLISH READERS

General Editor: D. H. Howe

Journey to the Centre of the Earth

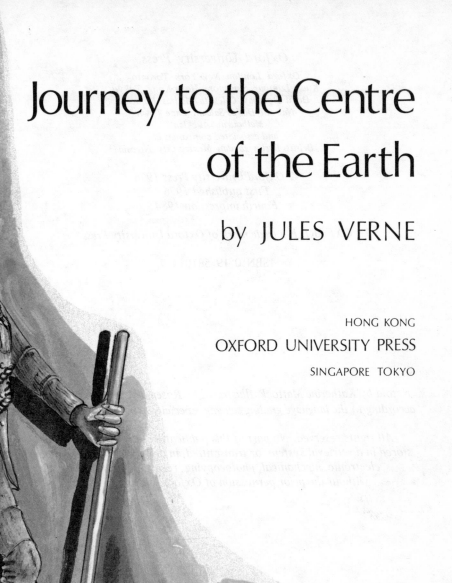

Journey to the Centre of the Earth

by JULES VERNE

HONG KONG

OXFORD UNIVERSITY PRESS

SINGAPORE TOKYO

Oxford University Press

Oxford London New York Toronto
Kuala Lumpur Singapore Hong Kong Tokyo
Delhi Bombay Calcutta Madras Karachi
Nairobi Dar es Salaam Cape Town
Melbourne Auckland
and associated companies in
Beirut Berlin Ibadan Mexico City Nicosia

© Oxford University Press 1976
First published 1976
Fourth impression 1984

OXFORD is a trade mark of Oxford University Press

ISBN 0 19 581014 7

Retold by Katherine Mattock. Illustrated by Rosemary Parsons. Simplified
according to the language grading scheme especially compiled by D.H. Howe

Printed in Hong Kong by Nordica Printing Co.
Published by Oxford University Press, Warwick House, Hong Kong

Contents

Oxford Progressive English Readers Language Scheme

The OPER language grading scheme was especially compiled by D. H. Howe as a guide to the preparation of language teaching material for school pupils and adults learning English as a second or foreign language. The scheme provides lists of words and language structures subdivided into three grades of difficulty and meant to be used in conjunction with each other.

The items were chosen according to two main principles: first, that they are likely to have been learnt or at least encountered *before* the stage indicated; second, that they are frequently occurring and useful, necessary to express a wide range of ideas, and difficult to replace with simpler words or constructions.

Use of the scheme is intended to eliminate unnecessary difficulties of language which would otherwise hinder understanding and enjoyment.

1 The Mysterious Parchment*

On 24 May, 1863, which was a Sunday, Professor Lidenbrock came rushing back to his little house on King's Street, one of the oldest streets in the old part of Hamburg.

Martha had only just started cooking lunch.

'If my uncle is hungry,' I said to myself, 'he'll be very 5
cross. He's the most impatient man.'

'Is Professor Lidenbrock here already?' cried poor Martha, half-opening the dining-room door.

'Yes, Martha, but don't worry if lunch isn't cooked. The clock has only just struck half-past one.' 10

'Then why is the Professor coming home? Here he is! I'm going, Mr Axel. You'll explain to him, won't you?'

Good Martha went back to her kitchen and I was left alone. But I'm not the sort of man who can calm impatient professors. I was about to creep upstairs to my room when the 15
street door creaked open, footsteps shook the staircase and the master of the house rushed straight through the dining-room into his study.

On his way, he threw his walking-stick into a corner, and his wide hat on to the table. He said to me, 'Axel, follow 20
me!'

Before I could move, the Professor called again, 'You're not here yet?'

I rushed into my master's study.

Otto Lidenbrock was not a bad man, I must admit, but he 25
was becoming more and more unusual.

He was a professor at the Johannaeum and gave lectures on mineralogy*, during every one of which he lost his temper.

Unfortunately, my uncle did not speak well in public. In these lectures he would often stop suddenly, struggling with a 30

---

*parchment, animal skin used instead of paper.
*mineralogy, the study of rocks and substances found in the earth.

difficult word which, when it finally came out, came out as a swear-word.

Now in mineralogy there are many difficult phrases, half Greek and half Latin. Even a good speaker might have
5 difficulty with them but every time it happened to my uncle, he flew into a rage.

This weakness of his was well known. The students waited for the difficult passages where he lost his temper and then burst out laughing — which isn't polite, even in Germany. So,
10 although many people attended the Lidenbrock lectures, it was only because they liked to laugh.

Nevertheless, my uncle was a real man of learning, a geologist* and mineralogist who could instantly say to which of the 600 known species* any mineral belonged.
15 The name of Lidenbrock was mentioned with respect in all colleges and learned societies. Men like Humboldt and Humphry Davy never failed to visit him when they came through Hamburg and famous chemists would discuss with him their most difficult problems.
20 This, then, was the gentleman who was calling me so impatiently. Imagine a tall thin man, in excellent health and with a fair skin which made him look much less than his fifty years. His big eyes rolled behind his huge glasses and his long thin nose looked like the blade of a knife.
25 When I add that he took steps exactly three feet long and that he kept his fingers tightly closed as he walked — a sure sign of a man with a temper — you will know enough not to want him as a companion.

My uncle lived quite well for a German professor. The
30 little house on King's Street was built half of brick and half of wood, overlooking a canal. It belonged to him and so did its contents — which included his 17-year-old god-daughter*, Mary from the Virlande, our good Martha and myself. I, being both his nephew and an orphan*, was his assistant.

*geologist, a man who studies rocks.
*species, group.
*goddaughter, a child the godfather promises to care for at Christian
        baptism, not usually a relative.
*orphan, a child whose parents have died.

I loved my work, I must say. I was a born mineralogist. My stones never bored me.

Altogether, life was happy in that little house on King's Street, in spite of the master's bursts of bad temper. But the man could never wait, he was always in a greater hurry than 5
Nature. In April, after he had planted flower seeds in pots in his room, he would pull their leaves every morning to make them grow faster.

Such a man had to be obeyed. I therefore rushed into his study. 10

An exciting discovery

That study of his was like a museum. Specimens* of every mineral could be found there, carefully labelled and arranged in the right class.

How well I knew them! How often, instead of wasting my time playing with boys of my own age, I had dusted them. 15
The coal and the metals, from iron to gold! And all those stones, enough to rebuild the whole King's Street house and even add a splendid room for me!

But as I went into the study, my thoughts were on my uncle, not on these wonders. 20

He was sitting in his big armchair, admiring a book with covers of coarse leather.

'What a book!' he was saying. Professor Lidenbrock loved unusual books. 'A priceless treasure that I found this morning in the old bookshop!' 25

'Splendid!' I replied, pretending to be interested. Why was he so excited about an old book?

'Yes, it's splendid! And does it open easily? Yes. Does it close well? Yes. Look at the back — not a crack in it after 700 years!' 30

'And what's the title of this wonderful book?' I asked with false eagerness.

'This book,' replied my uncle with increasing excitement, 'is by Turleson, the famous Icelandic writer of the twelfth

specimen, example.

century! It is his story of the Norwegian princes who ruled
Iceland.'

'I suppose it's a translation,' I cried as brightly as I could.

'What!' roared the Professor. 'A translation? This is the
5   original work, in that magnificent language Icelandic.'

That surprised me a bit. 'Is it well printed?' I asked.

'Printed! You think it's a printed book, do you? It's a
manuscript*, you foolish boy, a Runic manuscript.'

'Runic?'

10   'Yes. Now I suppose you want me to explain that. Runes
are the letters of an alphabet that was used long ago in Iceland. Look at them, boy, and admire – '

At this point, a dirty piece of parchment fell out of the
book on to the floor. My uncle seized it.

15   'What's this?' he cried, carefully unfolding it on his table.
The parchment contained a few lines of strange letters. These
are the letters that caused Professor Lidenbrock and his
nephew to make the strangest expedition of the nineteenth
century.

20   The Professor looked at the letters for a few moments.
Then, lifting his glasses, he said, 'These are Runic letters.
They are exactly the same as those in Turleson's manuscript.
But what do they mean? It must be old Icelandic.'

Professor Lidenbrock didn't know all the 2,000 languages
25   used in this world but he knew very many of them. If he
couldn't understand this one, he would certainly lose his
temper. I was waiting for it to happen when the little clock
over the fireplace in the study struck two o'clock.

At that moment, Martha opened the door saying, 'The
30   soup is ready.'

'Soup! Don't bother me with soup!' shouted my uncle.

Martha ran. I ran after her and somehow found myself sitting in my usual place in the dining-room.

I waited for a few minutes. The Professor didn't come. He
35   had never missed his lunch before. And what a lunch! Soup,
eggs, meat and fish, served with an excellent German wine.

*manuscript, a handwritten document.

My uncle was going to miss all this because of a piece of old paper! I was his nephew. It was my duty to eat for him as well as for myself, and I did so.

'Professor Lidenbrock not at the table!' said Martha, 5 shaking her head. 'It means something serious is going to happen.'

I didn't think it meant anything, except perhaps trouble because I had eaten my uncle's lunch.

I had just finished when a voice roared. I leapt from the 10 dining-room to the study.

Saknussemm's puzzle

'It's definitely Runic,' said the Professor, frowning, 'and I intend to find out what it means. Sit down and get ready to write.'

I was ready.

15 'Now, I am going to call out to you the letters of our alphabet that match these Runic letters. We'll see if that solves it. Make no mistakes, I warn you!'

I was as careful as I could be. He called out the letters one after another and together they formed three strange words.

20 My uncle seized the paper on which I had written and studied it for a long time.

'What does it mean?' he kept asking himself. 'It's a puzzle in which the letters have been purposely mixed up. Just think! In their correct order, they may be a hint which will 25 lead us to some great discovery!'

I doubted it but, sensibly, I didn't say so to my uncle.

The Professor compared Turleson's manuscript with the piece of parchment. 'The writing is different,' he said. 'And that double *m* at the beginning wasn't used in Iceland until 30 the fourteenth century. So the puzzle is at least 200 years later than the book. I think one of the owners of the book must have composed it. But who was he? Surely he wrote his name somewhere on the manuscript?'

My uncle lifted his glasses and examined the opening pages

of the book through a magnifying glass*. On the back of the second page, he found a few faded letters.

'Arne Saknussemm!' he cried triumphantly. 'That's the name of a famous Icelandic alchemist* of the sixteenth century. Those alchemists, they made amazing discoveries. Why, 5 Saknussemm may have hidden some discovery in this puzzle. Yes! YES!'

The Professor was excited by the idea.

'But why should a scientist want to hide a wonderful discovery in this way?' I asked. 10

'Why indeed? That's what we're going to find out. I shall neither eat nor sleep until I understand this piece of parchment. And nor shall you, Axel,' he added.

'Good Lord!' I thought. 'I'm glad I ate two lunches today.'

'First,' said my uncle, 'we must try to find the key to the 15 code*. That should be easy. The words on the parchment contain so many vowels that they must belong to one of the southern languages of Europe, not northern. Saknussemm was an educated man. When he was not writing in his own language, he would have written in Latin. So, this is Latin but 20 Latin in a mixed-up form.'

'Well,' I thought to myself, 'if you can unmix it, my dear uncle, you are a clever man.'

'Let us study it,' he said, picking up the piece of paper on which I had written. 'Here are 132 letters, Axel.' 25

But I was looking at a charming picture on the wall, a picture of Mary. My uncle's god-daughter was staying with a relative at Altona and her absence made me sad for — I now confess — Mary and I loved each other and were secretly engaged*. Mary was a pretty girl with blue eyes and fair hair 30 who was rather solemn but loved me nevertheless. I worshipped her and the picture of her carried me into a world of dreams.

*magnifying glass, glass which makes objects appear bigger.
*alchemist, scientist of the Middle Ages.
*code, secret writing.
*engaged, going to be married.

I remembered my faithful companion. Every day, Mary used to help me arrange my uncle's precious stones. What pleasant hours together! And how I envied those unfeeling stones she handled with her dear fingers!

5   Then, when our work was finished, we used to walk hand in hand to the banks of the River Elbe.

My uncle banged the table, interrupting my dream.

'Axel!' he said. 'Perhaps all we need to do is to write down the first letter of each word, then the second letter, then the

10   third . . . '

Professor Lidenbrock's eyes flashed behind his glasses. His fingers trembled as he picked up the old parchment. He coughed loudly and solemnly read out to me the first letter of each word, then the second letter and so on until I had

15   written more nonsense words.

I admit that, by now, I was excited myself. I expected the Professor to read out a magnificent Latin sentence.

To my surprise, his hand struck the table. The ink splashed and the pen flew out of my hand.

20   'That can't be right!' shouted my uncle. 'It makes no sense!'

He rushed across the study, down the stairs and out on to King's Street as fast as his legs would carry him.

2 I Find the Key

'Has he gone?' cried Martha, running out of her kitchen as the street door banged. 'What about his lunch?'

'He won't eat it,' I replied.

'And his supper?'

'He won't eat that either, Martha. Uncle Lidenbrock is not 5
going to eat, and nor is anybody else in this house, until he understands some old puzzle that never will be understood.'

'Oh dear! You mean we shall have to die of hunger?' The old servant went unhappily back to her kitchen.

I thought of going to tell Mary. But the Professor might re- 10
turn at any moment. If he called me and I didn't answer, what might happen then?

It would be wiser to stay. I started working on a new collection of stones that had arrived from France but my head ached and I sensed that something terrible was going to 15
happen.

After an hour, the collection was arranged. I sat in my uncle's chair and lit my pipe. Where was the Professor now? Would he return in triumph or despair? I picked up the paper on which I had written the letters. 20

'What can it mean?' I muttered.

I tried grouping the letters to form words. It was impossible! Although I could find one or two English words and Latin words and French words, I could find no connection between them. 25

As I struggled, my brain got heated, my eyes blinded. I was choking. I needed air. Without thinking, I started fanning myself with the piece of paper. Imagine my surprise! As the back of the paper was turned towards me, I thought I could read more Latin words. 30

Suddenly, I understood. I had found the key to the puzzle! The paper could be read just as it was. The Professor had been right: right about the language, right about the arrangement of the letters. Now, chance had shown me how to read them!

I spread the paper out on the table so that I could read it
5   at a glance. I calmed myself by walking twice around the room. Then I dropped into the armchair and took a deep breath.

'Now let's see what it says,' I said to myself.

I bent over the table. Putting my finger on each letter in
10   turn, I read aloud the whole message.

What terror it produced! Had some man dared to go into —

'Oh no!' I cried, jumping up. 'My uncle mustn't know about this. If he heard about such a journey, he would want to do it too. Nothing would stop him and he would take me
15   with him and we should never come back. Never! Never!'

I was more upset than I can say.

'If my uncle keeps on thinking about this puzzle,' I declared, 'he too may discover the key. So I must destroy it.'

A small fire was still burning in the study. I picked up the
20   paper and Saknussemm's parchment. I was about to throw them both on to the fire when my uncle opened the door.

I tell the Professor

I only just had time to put the papers back on the table.

Professor Lidenbrock seemed to be able to think of nothing except the puzzle. He sat straight down in his chair,
25   picked up his pen and worked at a mathematical solution for three long hours. He didn't speak, he didn't lift his head. He rubbed out, he crossed out, he started again hundreds of times.

At first, I trembled in case he solved it. But so many different
30   combinations of the letters were possible that there was really no danger.

Night came. The noises in the street stopped. My uncle saw nothing and heard nothing, not even Martha asking, 'Are you going to have any supper tonight, sir?'

35   Poor Martha went away unanswered, and I fell asleep.

When I woke up next morning, the Professor was still working. His eyes were red, his cheeks were pale, his hair was a mess.

I honestly felt sorry for him but I did not say the word that could have ended his suffering. I was not a cruel man. *5* Why did I not speak? To protect him.

'I know him,' I said to myself. 'He would want to go. Nothing would stop him. He would risk his life to do something no other geologist has done. If I told Professor Lidenbrock how to read the parchment, it would be the same *10* as killing him. Let him find out for himself if he can.'

And so I waited. But I had forgotten about my stomach.

Martha could not go to the market as the Professor had locked the street door and removed the key. So there was no breakfast. I decided to be strong. *15*

At midday, I still stood firm. But by the time two o'clock came, I felt really hungry. I started telling myself that the parchment was not so important, that my uncle would treat it as a joke, that he could be stopped from going, that I might as well tell him the secret as wait for him to discover it . . . *20*

At that point in my thoughts, the Professor stood up and put on his hat. What! Were Martha and I still to be locked in?

'Uncle!' I said. 'Uncle Lidenbrock!'

'Eh?' he said, like a man suddenly woken up.

'What about that key?' *25*

'What key? The key to the door?'

'No,' I cried, 'the key to the puzzle!'

The Professor looked at me over the top of his glasses, then seized my arm. His hand became tighter and tighter until I had to speak. *30*

'Read that,' I said, handing him the paper on which I had written. 'Read it backwards.'

The Professor cried out. He understood.

Seizing the paper with tears in his eyes, he read out the whole message from the last letter to the first. *35*

It was poor Latin but it can be translated into English

thus:

> *Go down into the crater* of Sneffels Yokul,*
> *Over which the shadow of Scartaris falls*
> *Before the first of July, brave traveller,*
> 5 *And you will reach the centre of the earth.*
> *I have done this. Arne Saknussemm.*

My uncle jumped as if he had received an electric shock. His joy was wonderful to see. He walked up and down, he held his head, he moved the chairs, he threw his precious
10 stones in the air. Finally, he fell into his armchair.

'What time is it?' he asked.

'Three o'clock' I replied.

'Is it really? I'm dying of hunger. Let's eat and after that . . .'

15   'After that?'

'You can pack my box.'

'What?'

'And your own,' said the Professor, going into the room.

I argue in vain

At these words, my whole body shook. To go to the centre
20 of the earth. What a crazy idea! But I decided to save my arguments for a suitable opportunity and gave all my attention to the business of eating.

I shan't repeat what my uncle said when he saw the empty table. I explained the reason and the door was unlocked so
25 that Martha could run to the market. She did well. An hour later my hunger was satisfied — and I remembered the situation.

My uncle told me to follow him from the dining-room back to his study.
30 'Axel,' he said quite gently, 'you are a very clever young man. You shall share the glory we are going to win.'

'He's in a good temper,' I thought. 'Now's the time to discuss that glory.'

'Above all,' my uncle went on, 'I insist on absolute secrecy. My rivals in the world of science must not hear about this journey until we return.'

**crater,* a large hole in the earth.

'Do you really think,' I asked, 'that there are many who would risk it?'

'Of course! There are many geologists who would rush after Saknussemm.'

'I'm not so sure, Uncle. We have no proof that Saknus- 5
semm actually did the journey. It might be a joke.'

'We shall see,' replied the Professor with a slight smile.

'But let me tell you all the possible objections,' I said.

'Speak out, my boy. You are now my partner.'

'Well, first, what do these names "Sneffels Yokul" and 10
"Scartaris" mean?'

'That is easy. Take down the atlas on the fourth shelf of the bookcase.'

I did so and my uncle opened it.

'Here is one of the best maps of Iceland. You can see that 15
there are volcanoes* all over the island and that they all have the name "Yokul". It means "glacier"* in Icelandic. Up there, most eruptions* take place through layers of ice.'

'But what is "Sneffels"?'

I was disappointed. He could answer that, too. 20

'Follow my finger along the west coast of Iceland. You see Reykjavik, the capital? Now follow it up farther and what do you see?'

'A piece of land that sticks out like a bone with a bump at the end.' 25

'Good. And can you see anything on that bump?'

'A mountain.'

'That is Sneffels. It is 5,000 feet high and will become the most famous mountain in the world if its crater leads to the centre of the earth.' 30

'But that's impossible!' I said, disgusted at such a silly idea.

'Impossible?' said Professor Lidenbrock sternly. 'Why impossible?'

'Because the crater must be full of lava* and burning rocks and —' 35

*volcano, mountain with openings through which gases and liquid rock come up from under the earth.
*glacier, river of ice.
*eruption, explosion from within the earth.
*lava, burning liquid earth and rocks.

'But Sneffels is a dead volcano. Its only known eruption was in 1229.'

I could not argue with that.

'What does "Scartaris" mean, then?' I asked. 'And why
5   does it say "the first of July"?'

My uncle thought for a few moments.

'Sneffels has several craters and Saknussemm had to show which one leads to the centre of the earth,' he answered. 'What did he do? He mentioned that just before July, the
10   shadow of one of the peaks of Sneffels, a peak called Scartaris, reaches the mouth of the right one. So, when we arrive at the top of Sneffels, we shall know exactly which way to go.'

Axel thinks the journey is impossible

My uncle had an answer to every question about Saknus-
15   semm's message. So I moved on to my more serious scientific objections.

'All right,' I said, 'I admit that the message is quite clear, I even admit that it doesn't seem to be a joke. Saknussemm went to Sneffels, he saw the shadow of one of its peaks touch
20   the edge of a crater just before July and he heard stories about that crater leading to the centre of the earth. But he didn't go down there and come back alive. Oh, no!'

'And why not?' said my uncle unpleasantly.

'Because it is generally recognized that the temperature
25   rises about one degree every seventy feet below the surface. At that rate, the temperature at the centre must be over two million degrees and everything there must be gas.'

'So it's the temperature that worries you, Axel?'

'Of course it is.'

30   'You are afraid of melting. Yet neither you nor anybody else knows what is happening inside the earth,' said Professor Lidenbrock scornfully. 'Why, at a certain depth, shouldn't the temperature reach its limit instead of rising to melting-point?'

I had nothing to say.

35   'After all,' he continued, 'scientists have proved that, if the temperature at the centre were two million degrees, the gases

produced would explode the earth's crust*. And it is a fact
that the number of volcanoes has greatly decreased since the
beginning of the world. Is it not therefore likely that, if there
is heat at the centre, it too is decreasing?'

'Likely perhaps, Uncle, but not proved.'   5

'But the greatest scientists agree with me. Do you remember when the famous English chemist Humphry Davy visited
me in 1825?'

'No, I don't. I wasn't born until 1844.'

'Well, Davy showed me, here in this room, that the earth is   10
heated by the combustion* of its surface and nothing else.
He wetted a metal ball with light rain — and an eruption took
place that made the ball too hot to hold.'

I began to be shaken by the Professor's arguments.

'My own opinion,' he added, 'is that the central heat you   15
believe in, doesn't exist. However, like Arne Saknussemm, we
shall see. But keep quiet about all this, so that nobody tries
to reach the centre of the earth before us.'

*earth's crust, the surface of the earth.
*combustion, burning.

3 Getting Ready

I came out of my uncle's study in a fever. There was not enough air for me in the streets of Hamburg so I walked towards the banks of the river.

Did I believe what I had just heard? Did Professor Liden-
5 brock really mean to go to the centre of the earth? While he was talking, he had certainly carried me with him.

I should have liked to leave at once, without time to think.

But an hour later, I admit, my excitement died away and from the depths of the earth I rose again to the surface.

10 'It's too silly!' I exclaimed. 'It must be a mistake, a bad dream.'

I had walked round the town once following the river and now I reached the Altona road. Perhaps I might see Mary. Soon, sure enough, she came into sight, walking towards
15 Hamburg.

'Axel!' she said in surprise. 'You have come to meet me. That was nice of you.'

Then she saw my face.

'What's the matter?' she asked, holding out her hand.

20 Three sentences later, she knew.

For a few moments, she was silent. I don't know if her heart was beating like mine but her hand did not tremble. We walked on.

'Axel!' she said then. 'It will be a wonderful journey. The
25 right sort of journey for the nephew of a scientist.'

'What? Mary, you're not going to advise me against such an expedition?'

'No, my dear Axel. And I would gladly come with you both if I weren't a girl.'

30 How hard it is to understand women! This girl was en-couraging me to go on the expedition even though she was in love with me! And she would not have been afraid to come

herself. I was amazed and, to tell the truth, ashamed of myself.

'Still, it's a long time until the 1st of July,' I thought. 'My uncle may be cured by then of his desire to go underground.'

It was dark by the time we reached the house on King's   *5*
Street. I expected to find the place quiet, with my uncle in bed as usual. But I found him shouting and waving his arms among a crowd of men who were unloading goods on the path. Old Martha was running this way and that.

'Hurry up, Axel!' exclaimed the Professor as soon as he   *10*
saw me. 'You haven't packed, my papers aren't in order and I can't find the key to my bag.'

So it wasn't just a bad dream.

'Are we going then?' I whispered.

'Yes, of course, boy. At dawn the day after tomorrow.'   *15*
I ran to my little room.

There was no doubt about it. My uncle had been buying things for the journey. The path was covered with rope ladders and lamps and axes.

I couldn't sleep. Next morning, I was called early.   *20*

'My dear Axel!'

I came out of my room, thinking that my pale face and red eyes would win Mary's sympathy and change her ideas.

'Ah,' she said, 'I see that you feel better after a good night's rest.'   *25*

'Feel better?!'

'Axel,' Mary continued, 'I have had a long talk with the professor. He is a man of great courage and you must remember that his blood flows in you. He has told me about his plans and hopes. He will succeed, I am sure. Oh, Axel! What   *30*
glory there will be for Professor Lidenbrock and his companion! When you come back, you will be a man, his equal, free to speak and act as you wish, free to . . .'

Her face turned red and her words made me happier.

Still, I refused to believe we were leaving. I took Mary   *35*
along to the Professor's study.

'Uncle,' I said, 'I don't understand the hurry. It's only May 26 and . . . '

'You fool! Do you think it's so easy to get to Iceland from here? There is only one regular boat a month from Copen-
5 hagen to Reykjavik and it leaves on the 22nd.'

'Well?'

'Well, if we waited until June 22, we should arrive too late to see the shadow of Scartaris touch the crater. So we have to get to Copenhagen as fast as we can, to find some other ship.
10 Go and pack!'

I prepare to leave

I went back to my room. Mary came with me and packed everything I needed in a small box. She was so calm, so sensible that I nearly lost my temper with her. I went downstairs.

All day, instruments and guns had been arriving. Poor
15 Martha!

'Is the master mad?' she asked me.

'Yes,' I said.

'And he's taking you with him?'

'Yes,' I said.
20 'Where?' she asked.

I pointed towards the centre of the earth.

'Into the cellar?' exclaimed the old servant.

'No,' I said. 'Farther down than that.'

Night came. 'I'll see you tomorrow morning,' said my
25 uncle. 'We leave at six.'

I fell on to my bed. I dreamed wildly about abysses*. I felt the Professor's strong hand dragging me into deep pits. I kept falling. My life had become one long fall.

I woke up at five, worn out. I went down to the dining-
30 room. My uncle was at the table, eating a good breakfast. I looked at him with disgust but, as Mary was there, I said nothing. I ate nothing, either.

At half past five, a carriage* arrived to take us to the station at Altona. Soon it was filled with our luggage.

abyss, deep cut in the earth.
carriage, a horse-drawn vehicle.

My uncle solemnly handed over the keys of the house to Mary. She kissed her guardian calmly but could not stop a tear as her sweet lips touched my cheek.

'Go, Axel dear, go,' she said. 'When you come back, I shall be your wife.'   5

I held her in my arms and then got into the carriage. From the door, Martha and Mary waved goodbye. The driver whistled and the two horses galloped off along the road to Altona.

4 The Journey Begins

At half past six, the carriage arrived at the station and at seven o'clock we were sitting opposite each other on the train with all our luggage. The whistle blew and we were on our way.

I watched the changing scenery. My uncle checked his
5 pockets and bag to make sure he had brought all the right papers. I noticed the piece of parchment among them and cursed it from the bottom of my heart.

Three hours later, the train arrived at Kiel. From there, we went by ship and then another train to Copenhagen where we
10 arrived at ten in the morning on May 28 and went straight to a hotel.

After a hasty wash, the Professor was off again, taking me with him. Up and down the quays* we went, in search of a ship to Iceland.

15 I hoped we would not find one but I was disappointed: a little Danish ship, the *Valkyrie,* was sailing to Reykjavik on June 2. The Professor was so pleased that the captain was able to charge us double the usual fare. 'Come on board on Tuesday, at seven in the morning,' he said, putting the money
20 in his pocket.

'What luck!' said my uncle to me. 'Now let's have some breakfast and see the sights of Copenhagen.'

I explored the city like a child. What delightful walks we could have had there, my pretty Mary and I, beside the har-
25 bour and along the green banks. But Mary was far away and I would never see her again.

We practise climbing

My uncle, although he came with me, took no notice of the royal palace or any of the usual sights. But he did get excited about a certain church spire* in the south-west district
30 and we went by boat along the canals to examine it.

*quay, place where ships are tied up.
*spire, tall, pointed part of a building.

To me, there was nothing remarkable about the church but
the Professor had seen an outside staircase winding round the
spire up into the sky.

'Let's go up,' he said.

'But we may get giddy*,' I protested.   5

'That's why we must go up. We have to get used to it.'

'All the same . . . '

'Come along. You're wasting time.'

The climb began. My uncle went quickly ahead, I followed
nervously.   10

While we were still inside, it was all right, but after one
hundred and fifty steps, fresh air struck me in the face. We
had reached the top of the tower. Now the outside staircase
began, protected only by an iron rail and with narrow steps
that seemed to rise into space without end.   15

*giddy, an unpleasant sensation in the head which causes one to lose
     one's balance.

'I can't do it!' I said.

'Coward! Come on!' replied the Professor.

I had to follow him, hanging on to the rail. I could feel the spire swaying in the wind. My legs grew weak. Soon I was
5 climbing on my knees, then my stomach. I shut my eyes.

At last, with my uncle dragging me up by my collar, I reached the ball at the top of the spire.

'Look,' he said, 'and look hard!'

I opened my eyes. The small clouds over my head seemed
10 still while the spire, the ball and I were being carried along at high speed. Far away, on one side, there was the green country and, on the other side, the glittering sea. The whole scene spun around beneath my eyes.

The Professor made me stand up straight and look around.
15 My first lesson had lasted an hour. When at last I was allowed to descend to the solid streets, I could scarcely stand at all.

'We'll do that again tomorrow,' said the Professor.

We climbed that spire every day for five days. And, in spite of myself, my performance improved.

We reach Iceland
20 The morning of June 2 arrived. By now we had letters of introduction to several important people in Reykjavik, including the Governor of Iceland.

Our precious luggage was taken on board the *Valkyrie* early.
25 'Is it a good wind?' my uncle asked.

'Couldn't be better,' replied the captain.

A few minutes later, the ship sailed out. In an hour she was through the straits between Denmark and Sweden and moving into the Kattegat.
30 'How long shall we take?' asked my uncle.

'About ten days,' the captain replied. 'As long as we don't run into a storm.'

'Would that delay us seriously?'

'Don't worry, Professor. We shall arrive in good time.'
35 Towards evening, the ship went round the northern point

of Denmark, and during the night, sailed along the southern coast of Norway and entered the North Sea.

Two days later, we sighted Scotland. Soon we reached the Atlantic and it was hard sailing.

I stayed well enough but my uncle, to his annoyance, was 5 sick from beginning to end. Instead of questioning the captain about Iceland, he had to stay in his cabin.

On June 11, we passed Cape Portland, the most southern point of Iceland. And on June 13, we anchored in Faxa Bay, off Reykjavik. 10

The Professor came out at last from his cabin, pale but as eager as ever. He dragged me forward and pointed at a high mountain with a double peak to the north of the bay.

'Sneffels!' he cried. 'Sneffels!'

We climbed down into a waiting boat and were soon on 15 Icelandic soil.

The first man we saw was the Governor. The Professor handed him his letters from Copenhagen and the Governor offered his ready help. My uncle was also kindly received by the Mayor of Reykjavik and Mr Fridriksson, a science-master 20 at the Reykjavik school. This delightful man took us to stay at his house.

'Well, Axel,' my uncle said to me. 'The worst is over.'

'Over?' I exclaimed.

'Why, yes. Now we have only to go down.' 25

'But when we have gone down, we still have to come up again.'

'Oh, that doesn't worry me.'

The Professor went to the library to look for Saknussemm manuscripts and I went out to explore the town. 30

It would have been difficult to lose my way in Reykjavik's two streets. In three hours I had seen everything there was to see, not only in the town itself but also around it. The views were particularly uninteresting. Faxa Bay to the west, shut in to the north by the Sneffels glacier. Lava and bare volcanic 35 rocks everywhere else. No trees and scarcely any plants. Just poor huts made of earth and peat*.

*peat, earth made of decayed plant material.

I met few people except on the main trading street where
they were busy loading fish. The men were strong but clumsy
and unsmiling, cut off from the rest of mankind in this land
of ice. The women were pretty but sad-looking. Like the men,
5   they wore dark clothes.

I returned to Mr Fridriksson's house, where I found my
uncle and his host together.

Help from the schoolmaster

Lunch was ready and Professor Lidenbrock ate well after
his unhappy days on board ship.
10   Conversation was in Icelandic but my uncle included some
German and Mr Fridriksson some Latin so that I should
understand.

'What books,' Mr Fridriksson asked my uncle, 'did you
hope to find in our library? I may be able to help you.'
15   I looked at the Professor. He hesitated about replying but
decided to speak.

'Mr Fridriksson,' he said, 'I want to find the works of Arne
Saknussemm.'

'Arne Saknussemm!' replied the Reykjavik teacher. 'You
20   mean the sixteenth century alchemist who was also a great
traveller?'

'Exactly.'

'One of the glories of Icelandic literature and science.'

'I see that you know him well.' My uncle was delighted to
25   hear his Saknussemm described thus. 'But what about his
works?'

'Oh, his works. We haven't got them.'

'What – not in Iceland?'

'Not in Iceland or anywhere else.'
30   'Why is that?'

'Because Arne Saknussemm was tried for heresy* and in
1573 his works were burnt at Copenhagen.'

'Excellent! Splendid!' cried my uncle, to the horror of the
Icelandic schoolmaster. 'That explains everything. Now I see
35   why Saknussemm had to hide his secret.'

*heresy, denial of the Church's teachings.

'What secret?' asked Mr Fridriksson.

'A secret which . . . whose . . . '

'Have you some secret Saknussemm paper?'

'No . . . er . . . no, I was just guessing.'

'I see,' said Mr Fridriksson and kindly changed the subject.   5
'I hope you won't leave our island without seeing some of its
mineral wealth.'

'No, indeed,' replied my uncle, 'but I imagine other scientists have been here before me.'

'They have, Professor Lidenbrock. But there is still plenty   10
to do.'

'Do you think so?' asked my uncle with an innocent air.

'Oh, yes. There are so many mountains and glaciers and
volcanoes still to be studied. Look at that mountain over
there, for instance. That is Sneffels.'   15

'Ah!' said my uncle. 'Sneffels.'

'Yes. One of the most interesting volcanoes, with a crater
which is seldom visited.'

'Is it dead?'

'It has been dead for five hundred years.'   20

'Well,' said my uncle, crossing his legs to stop himself from
jumping into the air. 'I think I should like to start my studies
with that Seffel . . . Fessel . . . What do you call it?'

'Sneffels,' replied the good Mr Fridriksson.

This part of the conversation had been in Latin so I had   25
understood it all. I could hardly stop myself laughing aloud at
my uncle's efforts to hide his delight.

'You have given me an idea,' he now told the schoolmaster.
'We shall try to climb that mountain and perhaps even study
the crater.'   30

'I am sorry that I can't accompany you,' said Mr Fridriksson.

'No! Oh, no!' my uncle replied quickly. 'Thank you very
much but we wouldn't wish to disturb you.'

'How do you expect to get to Sneffels, though?' asked our   35
host.

'By boat, I suppose, across the bay. That's the shortest
route.'

'That's not possible. There are no rowing-boats at Reyk-
javik. You will have to go by land, following the coast.'
'Good. I'll get a guide.'
'I can suggest one. A good, steady man. A hunter who lives
5   near Sneffels — and who speaks perfect Danish, too.'
'When can I see him?'
'Tomorrow, if you wish.'
'Why not today?'
'Because he won't arrive until tomorrow.'
10   'Tomorrow then,' sighed my uncle.

5 Our Guide Hans

When I woke up, my uncle was talking loudly in the next room. I got up and joined him.

He was speaking in Danish to a big, strong man with blue, intelligent eyes and long red hair. You could see at a glance that nothing could disturb such a man. He stood there with   5
his arms folded, unmoved by all my uncle's excited talk. When he wanted to say 'No', his head turned from left to right. When he wanted to say 'Yes', it bent forward so slightly that his long hair hardly moved.

I should never have guessed that such a man was a hunter   10
but Mr Fridriksson explained that he hunted only the eider* for her feathers and that the bird really did the work for him since she pulled out the feathers herself.

This hunter, called Hans, was to guide us to the village of Stapi at the bottom of Sneffels. We would start on June 16.   15
The journey would take seven or eight days. My uncle, myself and our luggage would go by horse. Hans would walk.

On arrival at Stapi, Hans would continue to work for my uncle as long as he was needed, on condition that he was paid three silver dollars every Saturday evening.   20

Never was an agreement reached so easily.

'A splendid character,' said my uncle as soon as Hans had gone.

'So he's coming with us to . . . .'

'Yes, Axel, to to the centre of the earth.'   25

It was already June 14 and we spent all day packing our things.

Instruments were put in one pack: thermometer*, manometer*, chronometer*, compasses*, telescope, lights. Guns were in another: two rifles, two revolvers. Tools were in a   30
third: axes, hammer, iron bars, ropes and rope ladders . . .

*eider, a kind of duck.
*thermometer, manometer, chrometer, compass, instruments for measuring temperature, pressure, time, and direction.

And food was in a fourth pack, enough food to last us for six months. The only liquid, however, was gin*. My uncle was taking no water. He expected to find underground springs.

In addition to all this, we had medicines, tobacco, money
5   and six pairs of tough, water-proof boots.

'We should be able to go a very long way,' said my uncle.

That evening, we had dinner with the Governor and Mayor. I couldn't understand a word that was spoken. I only saw that my uncle talked all the time.
10   The next day, June 16, we finished our packing. Mr Fridriksson, our host, gave my uncle a fine map of Iceland and we passed the evening in pleasant conversation with him. The night that followed was, for me, less pleasant.

At five in the morning, the sound of horses woke me. I
15   dressed quickly and went down into the street. There, Hans was skilfully loading the last of our luggage. My uncle was giving more advice than help and Hans took little notice of him.

At six, everything was ready. Mr Fridriksson shook hands
20   with us. My uncle thanked him gratefully in Icelandic. I thanked him in my best Latin. Then we mounted our horses. 'Go wherever luck leads you,' Mr Fridriksson called to me.

Slow progress

Hans, quick and untiring, walked ahead. The two pack-horses followed him and behind them rode my uncle and I.
25   Outside Reykjavik, Hans took a path along the coast. We rode between poor fields that were more yellow than green and saw nothing except a few cows and sheep. The hills to the east were hidden in mist. Now and then, patches of snow glittered on the slopes of distant mountains.
30   I smiled at the sight of my uncle, such a tall man, on his little horse.

'Good horse! Good horse!' he kept saying. 'You will see, Axel, that there is no animal more intelligent than the Icelandic horse. Snow, storms, rocks, glaciers — nothing can

*gin, a strong drink.

stop him. As long as we don't force him, we shall do thirty
miles a day.'

'*We* may, but what about the guide?'

'Oh, people like that can walk miles without even noticing
it.'   *5*

Two hours after leaving Reykjavik, we reached the little
town of Gufunes. Here, Hans stopped and shared our simple
breakfast, answering my uncle's questions about the road
with only a 'Yes' or 'No'.

It was now four o'clock and we had travelled twenty miles. *10*
The fjord* was over two miles wide at this point and the
waves crashed against its steep rocks.

'If these horses are really intelligent,' I said, 'they won't
try to cross.'

But my uncle tried to force his animal into the water with *15*
shouts and blows until, finally, it threw him off.

'There's a ferry,' said the guide in his usual Danish.

'Why didn't you say so before? Let's go,' said my uncle.

'Tide. We must wait,' said Hans.

My uncle stamped his foot impatiently. But it was six *20*
o'clock in the evening before the tide was right and it took
two men over an hour to row us across.

At half-past seven, we reached Gardär, where we were to
sleep for the night.

An Icelandic host

It was still light as, in Iceland during June and July, the *25*
sun never goes down. Nevertheless, the temperature had
fallen. I was cold and very hungry by the time we stopped at
a peasant's* house.

The master of the house shook hands and led us straight
along a passage to the visitors' bedroom which had a floor of *30*
beaten earth and two beds heaped with dry hay.

He invited us to join him in the kitchen, the only one of
the four rooms with a fire. When we walked in, the host and

fjord, narrow arm of the sea, between mountains (Scandinavian).
peasant, a poor farmer.

his wife said 'Be happy', kissed us on the cheek and bowed low. Their nineteen children crowded around and soon my uncle and I had three or four of them on our shoulders, as many more on our knees and the rest between our legs.

5   'Be happy! Be happy!' said all those who could talk.

And 'Be happy' said Hans who had just turned our horses loose for the night. Quietly, he kissed the host, his wife and their nineteen children.

Then the twenty-four of us sat silently down to supper. It
10   was strange food − dried fish and sour milk − but I was hungry and I ate and drank it all.

At last, I was able to get into my bed of hay.

At five o'clock next morning, we said goodbye to our host and gave him money that he didn't want to take.

15   Now the way became wetter and more lonely, with few animals and even fewer people. We crossed fjord after fjord and spent the night in an empty hut.

The scenery next day was the same but by night-time we were half of the way to Stapi.

20   On June 19, we walked on a floor of lava for a while but soon the ground was wet again beneath the horses' feet. We were travelling west now along the top of Faxa Bay and the two white peaks of Sneffels appeared in the clouds less than five miles away.

25   I was beginning to feel tired but my uncle stayed as fresh as the day we left Reykjavik. To our guide, of course, the journey was nothing.

On the evening of Saturday, June 20, we reached Budir village on the sea-shore where my uncle paid Hans as they had
30   agreed. We stayed the night with Hans's own family but next morning we rode on. We were very near Sneffels now and the Professor never took his eyes from it.

'So that,' he seemed to be saying, 'is the giant I am going to defeat.'

35   After four hours' walking, the horses stopped at the door of a cabin in Stapi.

Our last resting-place

Stapi is a village of about thirty cabins at the edge of a little fjord closed in by a strange and beautiful wall of natural rock columns, thirty feet high. But our cabin here, at our last resting-place on earth, was mean and dirty and our host a coarse peasant who drank too much. My uncle therefore *5* decided to start his great expedition as soon as possible and next day Hans arranged for three Icelanders (instead of the horses) to carry our things as far as the bottom of the crater.

Now my uncle had to explain to the guide that he intended to explore the inside of the volcano. Hans didn't mind. It *10* made no difference to him whether he went across his island or down into the heart of it. As for me, I had forgotten my fear during the excitement of the journey but now it seized me again.

Above all, I worried that Sneffels might not really be dead, *15* that a new eruption might at that moment be on the way. Finally I told my uncle what I feared.

'I've been thinking about that,' he replied simply.

Too good to be true! Was he actually being sensible? Was he thinking of giving up his expedition? *20*

'I've been thinking about that,' he repeated. 'Sneffels has been silent for six hundred years but it may speak again. However, there are always advance signs of an eruption. I have spoken to the villagers here and studied the ground and I can assure you, Axel, that there will be no eruption.' *25*

I was dumb with surprise.

'You don't believe me?' said my uncle. 'Then follow me.'

We left the cabin and walked through an opening in the rock wall, away from the sea. Here and there, among the huge volcanic rocks, I could see steam rising into the air. *30*

'You see the steam, Axel? It proves there will be no eruption.'

'I don't see how it proves that,' I said.

'Listen,' said the Professor. 'When an eruption is on the way, such steam increases greatly and the air becomes still *35* and heavy.'

'But . . . '

'Enough. When science has spoken, men should be silent.'

I returned to the cabin, feeling beaten. I had only one hope left: that when we reached the bottom of the crater, we
5 should find no passage.

I had a terrible dream that night, in which I was shot into space from the depths of a volcano.

The next day, June 23, Hans was waiting for us with three companions. To all our luggage, he had added one leather
10 bottle full of water. That, plus our own bottles, would give us enough water for a week.

It was nine o'clock in the morning. My uncle paid our coarse host all the money he demanded and we left Stapi.

6 Climbing Sneffels

Sneffels is 5,000 feet high. From our starting-point I could not see the two peaks against the grey sky. All I could see was a cap of snow.

Led by Hans, we walked one behind another along paths too narrow for two people. Conversation was more or less 5 impossible.

I had plenty of time to observe the country through which we were passing. The more I saw, the more confident I became. It was so clearly volcanic, so clearly the result of internal fires, that no fool would try to go below the surface. 10

The way became more and more difficult. The ground was rising. Pieces of rock kept breaking off, dangerously.

Hans walked over the rising ground as calmly as if it were level. Sometimes he disappeared behind great rocks and then a high whistle from him told us which way to go. 15

After three tiring hours, we had reached only the base of the mountain. Here, Hans ordered a stop and a little food was shared out for breakfast. My impatient uncle ate his quickly but the stop was meant for rest, too. He had to wait another hour before the guide gave the signal to continue. The three 20 Icelanders were just like Hans: they said nothing and ate very little.

Now we began to climb the slopes of Sneffels. The top seemed very close but how many hours it took to reach it! Loose stones kept rolling down at high speed. Sometimes, the 25 cliffs were so steep that we couldn't climb them at all and had to go around. We helped each other with our iron sticks at these difficult places. My uncle, I must say, stayed close to me and often gave me support. He seemed to have natural balance. The Icelanders, in spite of their heavy burdens, 30 climbed like real mountaineers.

Fortunately, after the first hour, a sort of volcanic staircase appeared through the snow. It served us well. By seven

in the evening, we had climbed the 2,000 stone steps of it to
the point where the Sneffels crater began.

The dust-storm

The sea stretched away 3,200 feet below us. We were
above the snow-line, which is not very high in Iceland. It was
5   cold and windy and I was very tired. My uncle, in spite of his
impatience, decided to stop and called the guide. Hans shook
his head.

'Higher,' he said.

'Why?' asked my uncle.

10   'Dust-storm,' said Hans.

'Yes, dust-storm,' repeated one of the Icelanders, in a
rather frightened voice.

'What's that?' I asked anxiously.

'Look,' said my uncle.

15   I looked down and saw a tall column of dust and sand
rising and twisting into the air. The wind was driving it towards our side of the mountain. The sun was hidden from
sight.

'Hurry! Hurry!' urged Hans.

20   We followed Hans as fast as we could. Soon the dust-storm
fell upon the mountain. Stones were picked up by it and fell
again like rain. If we had been caught, our bodies would have
been torn to pieces. Thanks to Hans, however, we were now
on the other side and sheltered from danger.

25   But the guide thought it unwise to spend the night there.
We continued our climb. Round and round, backwards and
forwards. It took us nearly five hours to climb the remaining
1,500 feet. I was weak from cold and hunger, and I could not
breathe properly at such a height.

30   At last, at eleven o'clock that night, in complete darkness,
we reached the top of Sneffels. Before sheltering inside the
crater, I saw the midnight sun shining on the island below.

The shadow of Scartaris

Supper was eaten rapidly and we settled down for the
night as well as we could. The bed was hard, there was not
35   much shelter and, at 5,000 feet above sea-level, the situation

was rather unpleasant. Yet I slept unusually well. I didn't
even dream.

Next day, we awoke half frozen by the sharp air, but in
bright sunshine. I got up from my stone bed to enjoy the
magnificent scene.   5

I was standing on top of the southern peak of Sneffels.
From that point, the view extended over most of Iceland.
Below me were deep valleys, lakes looking no bigger than
ponds, rivers no bigger than streams. To my right, in the east,
there were glaciers and snow-covered peaks, like waves on a   10
stormy sea. To my left, towards the west, stretched the ocean
itself. It was hard to see where the land ended and the water
began. I lost myself in wonder, delighted at the great height,
forgetting the abyss below.

Hans and the Professor joined me.   15

'Here we are at the top of Sneffels,' said my uncle, 'and
here are two peaks. Hans will tell us what Icelanders call the
one on which we are standing.'

'Scartaris,' said Hans.

My uncle looked at me triumphantly.   20

'Now for the crater!' he cried.

The crater of Sneffels was about one mile across at the
mouth. I estimated its depth at 2,000 feet but the bottom
measured not more than 500 feet all round, so the way down
was quite gentle.   25

I thought of the thunder and flames the crater had contained and might contain again. But I could not go back now.
Hans set off in front again, and I followed him without a
word.

We walked slowly down around the inside of the cone,   30
among the loose rocks. In some places, there were glaciers
and here Hans advanced with great care, using his iron stick
to test the ground. At certain points, we had to fasten ourselves together with a long rope so that, if one person slipped,
the others would save him.   35

By noon we had arrived. I looked up and saw the mouth of
the cone circling a patch of sky, with the peak of Scartaris
rising into space.

At the bottom of the crater there were three chimneys through which, during its eruptions, Sneffels had send out its lava and stream from the central furnace*. Each was about 100 feet across. I did not dare to look into them but Profes-
5   sor Lidenbrock ran rapidly from one chimney to the other, waving and muttering. The Icelanders and I sat on blocks of lava, watching. They clearly thought he was mad.

Suddenly my uncle shouted. I thought he had fallen in. Then I saw him with his arms stretched out in front of a
10   granite rock in the centre of the crater. He looked amazed, then wild with joy.

'Axel! Axel!' he cried. 'Come here! Come here!'

I ran over to him. The Icelanders didn't move.

'Look,' said the Professor.
15   Sharing his amazement if not his joy, I read on the rock the cursed name.

'Arne Saknussemm!' cried my uncle. 'Have you any doubts *now*?'

I didn't reply. Overcome by this piece of evidence, I re-
20   turned to my lava seat.

When I lifted my head again, only my uncle and Hans remained at the bottom of the crater. The three other Icelanders had been dismissed and were on their way back to Stapi.
25   Hans was sleeping peacefully under a rock while my uncle circled the bottom of the crater like a trapped animal. I had neither the desire nor the strength to get up so, like the guide, I went to sleep — but uneasily, imagining that the mountain trembled.
30   That was our first night inside the crater.

Next day, the sky over the cone was grey and cloudy. I noticed this not so much because of the darkness inside the crater but because of my uncle's anger.

I understood the reason for it, and hope grew again in my
35   heart. Let me explain.

Of the three ways open beneath our feet, Saknussemm had

furnace, intense fire.

taken only one – the one on which, according to the puzzle, the shadow of Scartaris fell during the last days of June. Now, if the sun failed to shine, there would be no shadow. It was June 25. If the sky remained cloudy for another six days,
5   the expedition would have to be postponed until next year.

The day went by and no shadow appeared on the bottom of the crater. Hans did not move from his place although he must have wondered what we were waiting for – if he ever wondered anything. My uncle did not speak to me once. He
10 looked only at the sky, in helpless anger.

On June 26, there was still no sun. It rained all day. Hans built a hut with blocks of lava and I quite enjoyed studying the noisy little waterfalls running down the inside of the cone. My uncle was desperate.
15 On June 27, the sky was still grey. But heaven always mixes joy and sorrow and Sunday, June 28, brought a change in the weather. The sun shone into the crater. Every rock and every stone had a shadow. The shadow of Scartaris stood out sharp as a blade and moved slowly with the sun.
20 My uncle moved with it.

At midday, it gently touched the edge of the middle chimney.

'It's there!' cried the Professor. 'It's there! Now for the centre of the earth!'
25 I looked at Hans.

'Forward!' said the guide calmly.

'Forward!' replied my uncle.

It was thirteen minutes past one.

7　Down the Chimney

The real journey was beginning. So far, it had just been hard work. From now on, there would be difficulties at every step.

I had not yet looked down into the pit but now the time had come. Hans was so calm that I was ashamed of my fear. I thought of my pretty Mary and walked across to the middle chimney. 5

I leaned over a rock and looked down. My hair stood on end. I started to sway. If Hans had not pulled me back, I should have fallen. Clearly, I had not taken enough lessons in heights at the church in Copenhagen. 10

All the same, I had seen the inside of the chimney for a moment. Its walls were almost vertical. Plenty of lava bumps stuck out for our feet to step onto but how should we balance? The staircase was there but the rails were missing! A rope fastened to the top of the chimney might help us on our 15 way down but what would happen when we came to the end of it?

My uncle solved the problem. He took a rope 400 feet long and as thick as a thumb, looped it over a block of lava and threw both ends down the chimney. We could each descend 20 holding both halves of the rope. When all three of us were 200 feet down, we could pull on one end of the rope and repeat the performance as often as necessary.

'Now,' said my uncle when he had finished, 'each of us will strap one pack on his back. Hans will take the tools. You, 25 Axel, will take the fire-arms, and I will take the delicate instruments.'

'But who,' I asked, 'is going to carry the clothes and this pile of ropes?'

'They will go down by themselves.' 30
'What do you mean?'
'You'll see.'

My uncle liked action. On his instructions, Hans tied the clothes and ropes in a single bundle and threw them down the chimney. I heard a loud rush of air. The Professor leaned over the edge, watching the bundle disappear from sight.

5   'Good,' he said. 'Our turn now.'

Was it possible to hear these words without terror?

We each strapped on our packs and the descent* began. Hans went first, then my uncle, then me. The silence was disturbed only by loose stones crashing into the abyss.

10   I let myself fall, seizing the double rope with one hand and steadying myself by my iron stick with the other. The rope seemed very thin to bear the weight of three people. I used it as little as possible and my feet gripped the lava bumps as if they were hands.

15   'Be careful!' said Hans quietly every time one of these slippery steps shook under his feet.

'Be careful!' repeated my uncle.

After half an hour we reached a rock that was firmly attached to the wall of the chimney. Hans pulled one end of

20   the rope and the other end came down from the top in a shower of stones and lava.

I still couldn't see the bottom of the hole.

Half an hour later we had descended another 200 feet by the same method.

25   No geologist, surely, would have tried to study the surrounding rocks at such a time. I certainly didn't. But the Professor seemed to be observing things for, at one stop, he said to me, 'The farther I go, the more confident I feel. These volcanic rocks show that Humphry Davy was right. I refuse

30   to accept the idea of central heat.'

He always came back to the same point and I felt no desire to argue. He mistook my silence for agreement, and the descent began again.

After three hours, I still couldn't see the bottom of the

35   chimney although the opening at the top was growing smaller all the time. It was gradually getting darker.

*descent, the climb down.

We had now thrown the rope fourteen times and each separate descent took half an hour plus quarter of an hour's rest. Altogether, that was 10½ hours. And fourteen descents with a rope 200 feet long: that meant we must be 2,800 feet down.   5

At that moment Hans called out, 'Stop!'

I stopped just before my feet hit my uncle's head.

'We have arrived,' said the Professor.

'Where?' I asked, slipping down beside him.

'At the bottom of the chimney.'   10

'Is there no other way out, then?'

'Yes, I can just see a sort of tunnel sloping away to the right. We'll look at it tomorrow. Let's have our supper first and sleep.'

It was not yet completely dark. We ate and lay down on a   15
bed of stones and lava. At the top of the chimney, as if at the end of a giant telescope, I could see a bright star. Then I fell into a deep sleep.

8 Ten Thousand Feet Below

At eight in the morning, a ray of daylight woke us up, reflected and multiplied by the lava walls. It was bright enough
for us to see surrounding objects.

'Well, Axel, have you ever spent a more peaceful night in
5 our little house on King's Street? No city noises here, eh?'

'Oh, it's certainly quiet enough down this well but it's also
rather frightening.'

'If you're frightened already,' cried my uncle, 'what will
you be like later? The pressure here is only twenty-nine
10 inches. This chimney only goes down to about sea-level. We
haven't so far gone a single inch into the earth itself . . . Now,
where is the bundle Hans threw down ahead of us?'

'Up there,' said the hunter, pointing to a bump about a
hundred feet above us. Easily as a cat, he climbed up to fetch
15 it.

'Good,' said my uncle. 'Now let us have breakfast. Remember, we may be going on a long journey.'

We swallowed our biscuits and meat with a few mouthfuls
of water mixed with gin.

20 Then my uncle took a little notebook out of his pocket.
He studied his instruments one after another, and recorded
the following information:

> *Monday, June 29*
> Time: 8.17 a.m.
25 Pressure: 29 inches
> Temperature: 6 °C
> Direction: East-south-east

The direction shown by the compass referred to the dark
tunnel my uncle had pointed out last night.

30 'Now, Axel,' exclaimed the Professor with pleasure, 'we
are *really* going to descend. This is the exact moment at
which our journey begins.'

With these words, he lit our two battery lamps and gave one of them to Hans to carry. Now we could see properly and would be able to for a long time.

'Forward!' cried my uncle.

Each of us picked up his own pack. My uncle entered the tunnel, followed by Hans pushing the bundles of clothes and ropes in front of him. I lifted my head and saw for the last time, at the top of the chimney, that Icelandic sky I was never to see again.

The tunnel sloped at about forty-five degrees. Fortunately, lava had forced its way along during the last eruption of 1229 and now this made useful steps under our feet. The lava shone, too, reflecting our electric light. On the walls, it formed coloured stalactites* and from the ceiling hung quartz* crystals like lamps that seemed to light up in welcome as we passed.

'It's magnificent!' I cried. 'What a sight, Uncle! Don't you admire the colours of that lava? And those crystals?'

'Ah, you're beginning to like all this, are you, Axel? Well, you'll see even finer sights, I hope. Quick march!'

It would have been more accurate to say 'Quick slide!' because we were simply slipping down steep slopes. The compass, which I kept looking at, pointed steadily south-east. The lava stream was like a straight line.

Yet the temperature was not rising much. I kept looking at the thermometer, too, and two hours after we entered the tunnel, it had only reached 10 °C. This made me think our descent was more horizontal than vertical — but the Professor would know, because he kept measuring.

At about eight in the evening, he ordered us to stop. The word 'stop' was music to my ears, we hadn't stopped for seven hours. Hans spread out some food on a block of lava and we all ate hungrily.

We were in a sort of cave where there seemed to be plenty of air, even gentle winds. I was too tired to think about it but one thing did worry me: our supply of water. My uncle was

*stalactites, rocky growth hanging from the roof of a cave.
*quartz, a hard mineral.

expecting to find underground springs but, so far, we had seen none.

'We have only enough water for five more days,' I told him.

5   'Don't worry, Axel. We shall find more water than we need as soon as we get beyond this lava.'

'But the lava may extend a long way. I don't think we have gone down very far yet.'

'Why do you say that?'

10   'Because if we had, it would be much hotter.'

'That's your idea,' replied my uncle, 'but what does the thermometer say?'

'Fifteen degrees, which means a rise of only 9 °C since we entered the tunnel.'

15   'So?'

'Well,' I said, 'the temperature underground is thought to rise one degree every 125 feet at least. Let us calculate from that.'

'Calculate it then my boy.'

20   'Easy,' I said, writing some figures in my notebook. 'Nine times 125 feet is 1,125 feet. So we have gone down 1,125 feet.'

'According to *my* observations,' said the Professor, 'we are 10,000 feet below sea-level.'

25   'Impossible!'

'Perfectly possible, or figures aren't figures any more!'

The Professor's calculations were correct: we had already gone 6,000 feet deeper than the deepest mines* in the world. Yet, instead of being over 80 °C, the temperature was only 30   15°. Very strange.

Up again

The next day, June 30, at six in the morning, we went on down the lava tunnel. It now sloped quite gently.

At 12.17, Hans stopped.

'Ah!' said my uncle. 'We have to make a choice.'

35   I looked around. The tunnel had divided into two narrow

*mine, area underground where men dig for minerals.

passages, both equally dark and narrow. Which should we take? It was difficult to decide.

My uncle did not wish to seem to hesitate. He pointed to the eastern passage and soon all three of us were in it.

The slope was now very slight. Sometimes, the passage opened up before us with tall arches like those of a church. Sometimes, it was so low we had to bend our heads or even crawl.

The temperature was still perfectly comfortable. How high it must have been, though, when the lava rushed along this route!

'I hope,' I thought, 'that the old volcano doesn't decide to start again while we're here.'

I didn't say anything to Uncle Lidenbrock. He wouldn't have understood my fears. His one idea was to go on, and he walked, slid and even fell with a determination I had to admire.

At six in the evening, after a fairly easy day, we had travelled five miles south but hardly quarter of a mile down. My uncle told us to stop. We ate without much conversation and went to sleep without much thought.

Our arrangements for the night were very simple: a blanket each, in which we rolled ourselves. After all, we had neither cold nor visitors to fear.

We awoke next day feeling fresh and cheerful, and continued our journey along the lava. The passage, however, was becoming horizontal. I thought it was perhaps even rising slightly. At about ten o'clock in the morning, we were definitely going up and I had walk more slowly.

'What's the matter, Axel?' the Professor asked impatiently.

'I'm tired.'

'What? When we've nothing to do except go down?'

'I'm sorry, Uncle, but you mean go up. The slope changed half an hour ago. If we go on like this, we shall return to the surface.'

The Professor shook his head, not wanting to hear. I tried to say more but he gave the signal to go on. I hurried after

Hans, who was following my uncle. It would be terrible to lose them.

Still, if we were going up we were getting nearer the surface. Soon I might see my little Mary again!

5   At noon, the walls of the passage changed. The lava was replaced by solid rock in sloping layers. We were leaving the granite! We were going the wrong way!

'Look!' I said to my uncle, pointing at the different kinds of rock.

10   'Well?'

'We have come to rocks of the period when the first animals and plants appeared.'

I made the Professor shine his lamp on the walls, expecting him to show surprise. He did not say a word. He simply

15   walked on.

Had he understood me? Did he refuse to admit he had chosen the wrong passage? It was clear that we had left the lava route and that this way could not lead to the furnace of Sneffels. Perhaps I was attaching too much importance to the

20   change in the rock. Perhaps I was making a mistake myself.

'If I *am* right,' I thought, 'I shall soon find some evidence of primitive* plants. I must keep my eyes open.'

Within a hundred yards, I found the proof I was looking for. We were no longer walking on lava but on a dust com-

25   posed of plants and shells. Professor Lidenbrock must have noticed but still he walked on.

I could not bear it any longer. I picked up the complete shell of a small animal and ran forward to my uncle.

'Look at this!' I said.

30   'Yes, it's a shell, Axel. We have left the granite and the lava route. I may have made a mistake but I cannot be sure until we reach the end of this passage.'

'I understand that, Uncle, and I would approve of going on – if we weren't in increasing danger.'

35   'What danger?'

'A shortage of water.'

'Then, Axel, we must drink less.'

primitive, very old.

9 The Search for Water

It was indeed necessary for us to drink less. Our supply of
water could not last more than three days, as I realized that
evening at supper.

All the next day, we walked almost without a word.

The rock glittered in the electric light and there were mag-   5
nificent specimens of coloured marble*. I noticed the fossils*
of more advanced creatures than I had seen yesterday. We
were climbing the ladder of animal life.

Professor Lidenbrock seemed not to notice. He was
waiting for one of two things to happen: for a gap to appear   10
at his feet down which we might continue our descent, or for
something to block our way. Evening came and neither hope
had been satisfied.

That night, I began to feel thirsty.

On the Friday, we set off again along the winding passage.   15
After walking for ten hours, I noticed that the marble and
other kinds of rock were being replaced by coal.

'A coal mine!' I exclaimed.

'A mine without any workers,' replied my uncle.

'Oh! Who knows?'   20

'*I* know,' replied the Professor. 'I am certain that this passage was not made by Man. It's time to eat. Let's have
supper.'

Hans prepared some food. I ate hardly anything but drank
the few drops of water I was allowed. Half the guide's bottle   25
was all the water that remained for three men.

My two companions stretched out on their blankets and
slept. I could not sleep and counted the hours until morning.

At six o'clock on the Saturday morning, we started again.
Twenty minutes later we reached a cave so huge that I rea-   30
lized this 'mine' could never indeed have been dug by Man.
We were, in fact, the first people ever to enter it.

*marble, a beautiful multi-coloured rock.
*fossil, a plant or animal which has turned to rock.

What a story those dark walls told! I thought about the period, all those millions of years ago, when coal beds were formed. I thought about all the mineral wealth we were passing through. I forgot to be tired.

5   This journey through the coal mine lasted until evening. My uncle became more impatient. We could never see more than twenty yards ahead, so we could never estimate the length of the passage.

Suddenly, at six o'clock, a wall appeared before us. To the
10 right, to the left, above or below, there was no way through. We had come to the end.

'Good!' cried my uncle. 'Now at least we know. We are not on Saknussemm's road and there's nothing we can do except turn back. Let us have a night's rest. In less than three days
15 we shall be back at the place where the tunnel divided.'

'Yes,' I said, 'if we have the strength.'

'And why shouldn't we have the strength?'

'Because by tomorrow we shall have no water.'

'And no courage either?' asked the Professor sternly.
20 I did not dare to reply.

'One more day'

We started early on the Sunday morning. By the end of the day, we had drunk all the water. After that, we had nothing to drink except gin, which burnt my throat so that I hated the sight of it. I was very tired. More than once I nearly
25 fainted. Then the others would stop and try to help me. But I could see that my uncle was suffering, too, from tiredness and thirst.

At last, at ten o'clock on Tuesday morning July 7, crawling on our hands and knees, we arrived back at the point
30 where the tunnel divided. I dropped onto the lava floor.

Hans and my uncle, sitting against the wall, tried to eat a few pieces of biscuit. I fell asleep.

After a while, my uncle came across and held me in his arms.
35 'Poor child!' he said kindly.

I was not used to tenderness from the stern Professor. I
seized his trembling hands in mine. He looked at me with
tears in his eyes, then he put his water-bottle to my lips.
'Drink,' he said.

Had I heard properly? Was my uncle crazy?   5

'Drink,' he said again, and I drank.

What sweetness I knew at that moment! Just one mouthful
of water but it was enough to save my life.

'Dear Uncle!' I whispered, with my eyes full of tears now.

'That's all there is, you understand. I kept it carefully at   10
the bottom of my bottle, Axel, I kept the water for you.'

'Thank you! Thank you!' I repeated, as some of my
strength came back. 'But now, Uncle, as we have no water,
we must return to Sneffels. May God give us the strength to
climb to the top of the crater again!'   15

'Go back?' said my uncle, almost to himself.

'Yes, go back. Immediately.'

There was rather a long silence.

'So, Axel,' said the Professor in a strange voice, 'that water
I gave you didn't bring back your courage and energy?'   20
What sort of man was this?

'What, you don't want to return?'

'And give up this expedition, just when it may succeed?
Never!'

'Then we must be prepared to die?'   25

'No, Axel, no. You must go back. I don't want you to die.
Hans will go with you. Leave me here alone.'

'Leave you here!'

'Leave me, I tell you. I have started this journey and I shall
either finish it or never return. Go, Axel, go!'   30

The guide followed this scene with his usual lack of con-
cern. He must have understood what was going on from the
different ways my uncle and I were pointing but he seemed
uninterested, even though it affected his life. He was ready to
leave or stay as his master wished. How I wanted to be able   35
to explain to him! Together, we might have persuaded the
Professor to return to the heights of Sneffels. If necessary, we
might have forced him.

I went across to Hans and put my hand on his. He did not move. He knew my suffering but the Icelander gently shook his head and calmly pointing to my uncle, he said, 'Master.'

'Master?' I cried. 'You're mad. He isn't the master of your
5 life! We must go back! We must take him with us! Do you hear me? Do you understand?'

I had seized Hans by the arm and was trying to make him get up, when my uncle interrupted.

'Calm yourself, Axel,' he said. 'Hans is too faithful a ser-
10 vant to do what you ask. So listen to what I suggest.'

I folded my arms and looked straight at my uncle.

'The lack of water,' he said, 'is our only problem. In the eastern passage of lava and coal, we found none at all. If we follow the western passage, we may be more fortunate.'
15 I shook my head as if I couldn't believe what I heard.

'Let me finish,' the Professor went on. 'While you were lying here asleep, I looked at that western passage. It goes straight down. In a few hours, it will bring us to granite and there we are sure to find plenty of springs. I know it, and I
20 am asking you for only one more day. If, after one day, I have not found the water we need, I swear to you that we shall all return to the surface.'

What an effort it must have cost my uncle to make such a promise! I could not resist him.
25 'All right,' I said, 'do as you wish, and may God reward your extraordinary energy. You have only a few hours left. Let's go!'

'I'm dying!'
The descent began again, this time by the western passage. Hans went first as usual. We had not walked a hundred yards
30 before the Professor, shining his lamp along the walls, cried, 'These are primitive rocks! *Now* we are on the right path! Forward!'

The twisting passage we had entered was formed in the early days when the earth was cooling down and shrinking
35 into gaps and hollows.

The further down we went, the more clearly the primitive
layers of rock appeared. What a chance for a mineralogist! To
see such rocks in position, to be able to touch them!

Through the layers of rock, touched with splendid shades
of green, we could see threads of copper and occasional gold.   5
Riches hidden for ever from the greedy eyes of men!

Next we came upon glittering white mica*. So bright was
the light reflected from our lamps that I felt as if I were walking inside a diamond.

At about six o'clock in the evening, this festival of light   10
came to an end. The walls grew darker. The mica joined with
other minerals to form the hardest rock of all, the rock that
carries the weight of the whole earth. We were in a huge
prison of granite.

It was now eight o'clock and there was still no sign of   15
water. I was wild with thirst. My uncle marched on, listening
always for the sound of a spring. My legs began to fail. I tried
to keep walking so that he should not have to stop. That
would drive him to despair for the day was nearly over — the
last day that he had.   20

But finally I cried out and fell.

'Help! I'm dying!'

My uncle turned back. He looked down at me with his
arms folded.

'It's all over,' he muttered.   25

His expression of rage was the last thing I saw before I
closed my eyes.

When I opened them again, I saw my two companions lying
rolled up in their blankets. Were they asleep? I could not
sleep, I was suffering too much. My uncle's words — 'It's all   30
over!' — echoed in my ears. There was no remedy. I was so
weak there was no hope of returning to the surface.

We had four miles of the earth's crust above us and all its
weight seemed to be on my shoulders. I felt crushed as I tried
to turn on my granite bed.   35

A few hours passed. There was a deathly silence. No sound
could reach us through walls so thick.

*mica, a mineral.

Yet I thought I heard a noise. It was growing darker in the passage and I thought I saw the Icelander disappearing with his lamp.

Why was he leaving us? Was he abandoning us? My uncle
5 was asleep. I tried to shout but no sound came through my dry lips. It was now completely dark, and silent again.

'Hans has abandoned us!' I cried to myself. 'Hans! Hans!'

After my first fright, I felt ashamed of suspecting such a man. And in fact, Hans was not going back up the passage,
10 he was going farther down it. Had he discovered something? In the silence of the night, had he heard something that I had not?

10　We Find Water

For a whole hour I tried to decide why our quiet hunter had left us. The strangest ideas entered my mind. I thought I was going mad.

At last I heard footsteps deep down. Hans was returning. A light began to shine on the walls and then came round the nearest corner. Hans appeared. 5

He went over to my uncle, put his hand on his shoulder and gently woke him up.

'What is it?' asked my uncle.

'Water,' said Hans. 10

'Water! Water!' I cried, clapping my hands and waving my arms as if I really were mad.

'Water!' repeated my uncle. 'Where?'

'Down below,' replied Hans.

Down below! I squeezed the guide's hands in thanks, while 15 he looked calmly at me.

We got ready quickly and were soon going down a steep hill. Half an hour later, we had travelled a mile and a quarter and were 2,000 feet deeper into the earth. We had found no spring and I was frightened again. 20

At that moment, I heard a sound like distant thunder through the granite walls.

'Hans was not mistaken,' said my uncle. 'That noise is the roar of a river.'

'A river?' I asked. 25

'No doubt about it. An underground river is flowing around us.'

We hurried on, full of hope. I no longer felt tired. The sound of running water had already refreshed me. The river, which had been over our heads, was now leaping along inside 30 the wall on our left. I kept touching the rock to see if it were wet but I could feel no water.

Another half an hour passed. We had walked another mile and a quarter.

We realized that the guide had gone no further than this during his absence. He had sensed the presence of water in 5 the rock but he had not seen it or drunk it.

We also realized that the noise of the water was getting fainter. If we went any further, we should leave it behind.

We turned back. Hans stopped at the point where the river seemed closest. I sat near the wall. I could hear water rushing 10 violently past about two feet away but a granite wall still separated us.

Hans makes a hole in the wall

I sighed heavily, without trying to think of any solution. Hans looked at me and I thought I saw him smile. He stood and picked up his lamp. He went up to the wall. He pressed 15 an ear against the dry stone and moved it slowly backwards and forwards, listening hard. I realized that he was trying to find the exact spot where the noise was loudest. He found that spot three feet above the ground. Excited, I hardly dared to guess what the guide intended to do.

20 He seized his axe, and I knew.

'We are saved!' I cried.

'Yes,' said my uncle, equally excited. 'Hans is right! What a splendid servant he is!'

Nothing, of course, could be more dangerous than to use 25 an axe. This rock supported the world. What if the wall fell and crushed us? What if the water, bursting through the rock, carried us away? These were real dangers but, at that moment, we were so thirsty we didn't care.

My uncle and I would have been in too much of a hurry 30 to strike the rock properly. Hans was calm and controlled. He struck it lightly until there was an opening six inches wide. I imagined the water on my lips.

After an hour, the axe had gone two feet into the granite. I was twisting with impatience and my uncle was just picking 35 up his axe to join in, when water suddenly shot out of the hole.

Hans, almost thrown over by the shock, could not stop a cry of pain. When I put my hands in the water, I cried out, too. The spring was boiling hot!

'This water is boiling!' I protested.

5 'It will soon cool down,' said my uncle.

The passage was filling with steam and a stream was forming.

Soon we were able to drink. What pleasure! What joy! What was this water and where did it come from? We didn't
10 care. It was water and, although it was still warm, it brought us back to life. I drank without stopping, for a whole minute.

'There's iron in it,' I remarked then.

'Fine!' answered my uncle. 'This expedition will be as good for us as a holiday in a German spa*. I suggest we give Hans's
15 name to this health-giving stream.'

'Agreed!' I cried, and the stream was immediately named 'Hansbach'.

Hans didn't take any notice. After a short drink, he sat down in a corner in his usual quiet way.

20 'Now,' I said, 'we mustn't let this water run away.'

'Why not?' asked my uncle. 'I expect the supply goes on for ever.'

'Nevertheless,' I said, 'let's fill the bottles and try to stop up the opening.'

25 Hans, however, couldn't close the hole he had made in the wall. The pressure of water was too great.

'I've an idea,' said my uncle.

'What?'

'Why are we so anxious to close the hole?'

30 'Because . . . ' I could not actually think of a reason.

'Then let's allow the water to run on! It has to run downwards and it will guide us as well as refresh us as we go.'

'What a splendid idea!' I exclaimed. 'With the stream to help us, there's no reason why our expedition shouldn't
35 succeed.'

'So you're beginning to think like I do, my boy!' laughed the Professor.

*spa, a town where people go to drink health-giving waters.

'Not just beginning — I already do!'

'Wait a while, though. We need a few hours' rest before continuing.'

I had completely forgotten that it was night, although the chronometer now reminded me. Soon all three of us fell   5
pleasantly asleep.

11 Under the Sea

By the next day we had already forgotten all our sufferings.
At first I was surprised that I didn't feel thirsty and wondered
why. The stream running at my feet provided the answer.

We had breakfast and drank some of the healthy water. I
5 felt very cheerful. Why shouldn't a man as determined as my
uncle succeed with his expedition, when he had a guide as
hard-working as Hans and a nephew as loving as myself? If
anyone had suggested that I return to the top of Sneffels, I
should have certainly refused.

10 In any case, all we had to do was descend.

'Let us start!' I cried, waking up the oldest echoes in the
world.

We set off again at eight o'clock on Thursday morning,
July 9. The granite passage twisted and turned but the general
15 direction was always south-east. My uncle kept looking at his
compass to check.

The slope here was very slight. The stream ran gently beside us and I thought of it as a friendly goddess guiding us on
our way. I was merry – but my uncle wasn't. He cursed the
20 horizontal path, wishing it were vertical.

That day and next, we went a long way *along* but a very
little way *down.*

By the evening of Friday, July 10, we calculated that we
were seventy-five miles south-east of Reykjavik and seven
25 miles deep.

Suddenly, a frightening gap opened at our feet – what
geologists call a 'fault'. My uncle clapped his hands for joy
when he saw how steep it was.

'Now we shall make progress!' he cried, 'and without much
30 effort. The bumps in the rock make a proper staircase!'

Hans fastened the ropes safely around us and the descent
continued. I can't say it seemed dangerous: by now, I was
used to this sort of thing.

We went round and round, down a staircase that looked
man-made. Every quarter of an hour we had to rest, sitting
on some bump in the rock, talking as we ate and drank from
the stream. The Hansbach had turned into a waterfall but it
provided more than enough water for our thirst.   5

On July 11 and 12, still following the staircase, we went
another five miles into the earth's crust. Now we were about
thirteen miles below sea-level.

On July 13, the way became much easier, sloping gently
to the south-east at about forty-five degrees. As there was not   10
much scenery, it also became rather dull.

On Wednesday July 15, according to the Professor's calculations, we were eighteen miles underground and about
125 miles from Sneffels. When I heard this, I exclaimed in
surprise.   15

'What are you thinking, my boy?' he asked.

'I was thinking that, if your calculations are correct, we are
no longer under Iceland.'

'Is that so?'

'We can easily check.'   20

I looked at the map and made some measurements.

'I was right,' I said. 'We must have passed Cape Portland
and be south-east of Iceland under the sea.'

'Under the sea,' repeated my uncle, rubbing his hands with
delight.   25

'So the ocean is over our heads!' I exclaimed.

'Why, what could be more natural, Axel? Aren't there coal-
mines in the north of England that extend under the sea?'

The Professor might consider it natural but I didn't like
the thought of all that water over my head. Still, it didn't   30
make much difference whether it was mountains or sea on
top of us as long as the granite held out. I quickly got used
to the idea as the passage led us deeper and deeper to the
south-east. Soon we were very far down indeed.

Four days later, on the evening of Saturday, July 18, we   35
arrived in a huge granite hall. My uncle paid Hans his weekly
wages. The next day, it was decided, should be a day of rest.

A day of rest

So I awoke lazily on Sunday morning. We were now used to our life underground. I scarcely thought about sun or stars, about trees or towns any more. To us, living as fossils, these things were useless.

5   Our faithful stream flowed across the floor of the hall. We had travelled so far that its water was now cool enough to drink straight away.

After breakfast, the Professor decided to put his daily notes in order.

10   'When we get back to Germany,' he said, 'I want to be able to draw a map of our journey underground.'

'That will be very interesting, Uncle, but are your observations exact enough?'

'Yes, I have written down every angle and every slope. So,
15   first let us work out our exact position. Take the compass and tell me in which direction we've been travelling.'

I studied it.

'East by south,' I replied.

'Good,' said the Professor, making some rapid calculations.
20   'I estimate that we have travelled 213 miles from our starting-point.'

'So we are under the Atlantic Ocean?'

'Exactly.'

'And a storm may be raging above us? And ships may be
25   being thrown about on the waves?'

'Yes.'

'And whales* may be beating the roof of our prison with their tails?'

'Don't worry, Axel. They won't be able to shake it. Let's
30   think about our position again. We are 213 miles south-east of Sneffels and I estimate that we are forty-eight miles below the surface.'

'But scientists think that is the limit of the earth's crust!'

'I know.'

35   'And, if you're right, the temperature ought to be 1,500 °C.'

'*Ought* to be, my boy.'

*whale, the largest creature that lives in the sea.

'And all this granite ought to be melting.'

'Well, you can see that it is not melting. What does the thermometer say?'

'27·6°.'

'So the scientists are wrong by 1,472·4° and Humphry Davy was right. What do you say about that?'

'Nothing.'

I still believed in the theory of central heat, although I felt no heat myself. Perhaps the lava around the walls simply did not allow the heat to pass through. But I did not bother to argue. I just changed the subject.

'Uncle,' I said, 'at Iceland, the radius* of the earth is about 4,800 miles, isn't it?'

'Yes.'

'And we have done forty-eight of those miles.'

'Yes.'

'In about twenty days.'

'In about twenty days.'

'At that rate, it will take us 2,000 days to reach the centre! Nearly five and a half years!'

The Professor did not reply.

'Moreover, if we travel 213 miles horizontally for every 48 miles vertically, we shall come out at some point on the earth's surface long before we reach the centre!'

'Forget all your calculations!' retorted my uncle angrily. 'Another man has done this journey and I'm going to do it, too.'

'I hope so but . . . '

'Hold your tongue, Axel, and stop talking nonsense. Just look at the manometer. What does it say?'

'It shows there is considerable pressure.'

'Good. You can see that, by descending gradually, our bodies have got used to the breathing this air and thus we have avoided trouble.'

'Except for slight ear-ache.'

'That's nothing. You can stop it by breathing quickly.'

'Of course,' I replied, determined not to annoy my uncle

*radius, distance from the centre of a circle to its edge.

again. 'It's even a pleasure to live down here. Have you noticed how clearly we can hear?'

'I have.'

'But won't this density* increase?'

5   'It will. The density will increase and we ourselves will get lighter and lighter.'

'Then how shall we continue our descent?'

'We shall have to fill our pockets with stones.'

'You have an answer for everything, Uncle,' I replied 10   doubtfully.

There was one question my uncle would not be able to answer, however. Even if his Saknussemm had done this journey, since the manometer had not been invented at that time, how did he know when he had reached the centre of 15   the earth?

But I didn't ask this. We spent the rest of that Sunday in calculations and conversation. I agreed with everything the Professor said and I envied Hans his ability to go, without question, wherever he was led.

*density, thickness of the air.

12 Alone

Much steeper slopes now led us deep into the earth. Some days we advanced as much as four or five miles towards the centre. These were dangerous descents which we achieved only through Hans's skill and control. The calm Icelander helped my uncle and me through many situations which would have defeated just the two of us. 5

Day by day the guide became more silent, however, and so I think did we. Anyone shut up between four walls gradually loses the ability to put ideas into words.

More than two weeks passed. By August 7, we were 10 seventy-five miles down. We had seventy-five miles of rock, ocean, land and towns over us! We must have been about 500 miles from Iceland.

That day, the passage sloped very little. I was in front. My uncle had one lamp and I had the other, with which I was ex- 15 amining some granite.

Suddenly, turning around, I discovered I was alone.

'Well,' I thought, 'I was walking too fast, or Hans and my uncle have stopped somewhere. I must go back. Luckily, it's an easy climb.' 20

I walked back for quarter of an hour, but saw nobody. I called out, but nobody replied. My voice was lost in the echoes.

I began to feel uneasy.

'Keep calm,' I said aloud. 'There's only one path. I was in 25 front so I must go back.'

I climbed for another half an hour. I listened, in case anyone was calling me. In that density, sound travelled a long way. But the passage was strangely silent.

I could not believe I was alone. I could *not* be lost. And 30 even if I were, people who are lost always find their way again.

'As there's only one path and the other two are on it,' I
said to myself, 'I am certain to find them. All I have to do is
keep climbing. Unless, of course, they forgot that I was in
front and have turned back, too. But even then I shall catch
5 them if I hurry. Of *course* I shall.'

I only half-believed my own words. Besides, even these
simple ideas took me a long time to put together.

Then I wondered if I really had been in front. Yes, that
was certain. Hans had been following me, ahead of my uncle.
10 He had stopped to fasten his pack on his shoulders. It must
have been at that moment that I had gone ahead.

'Oh, in any case,' I remembered, 'there is my faithful
stream. All I need to do is follow it back up and I shall find
my companions.'

15 The thought cheered me up. How wise of my uncle to pre-
vent Hans from stopping up the hole in the wall! Having
supplied us with water for weeks, the stream would now be
my guide, too. I bent to wash in the Hansbach before continuing my climb.

20 To my horror, I found that I was standing on rough, dry
granite. The stream was no longer flowing at my feet!

Lost and in terror

To describe my despair at that moment is impossible. I was
buried alive. I would die twisted with hunger and thirst.

My hands passed over the granite floor. How hard and dry
25 the rock seemed!

Now I knew the reason for that strange silence when I had
listened for my companions' voices. But how had I lost the
stream? Clearly, the passage had divided and I had taken one
route while the Hansbach and my companions had taken the
30 other.

I was lost! Lost beneath seventy-five miles of rock! I felt
crushed.

I tried to think about things on the surface: about Hamburg, the house on King's Street and my poor Mary; about
35 our journey to Iceland, Mr Fridrikson and Sneffels. But what

human power could open the rock above me and take me
back there? Who could even show me the way back to my
companions?

'Oh, Uncle!' I exclaimed in despair.

I thought of asking heaven for help. Memories of my   *5*
childhood came back, and of the mother I had hardly known.
I knelt in prayer.

This calmed me slightly and I was able to think about my
situation.

My water-bottle was full and I had enough food for three   *10*
days. Should I go up or down? Up, of course, until I reached
the point where I had left the stream. Then, with the stream
at my feet, I might still be able to get back to the top of
Sneffels.

Why hadn't I thought of that before? Here was a chance of   *15*
reaching safety. I must find the Hansbach again.

Leaning on my iron stick, I started walking again. The
slope was rather steep but I felt hopeful, knowing I had no
choice. I tried to recognize my way by the slope of the rocks,
the arrangement of the bends but I could remember none of   *20*
it. Then after half an hour, the path came to an end. I
bumped into a wall of solid rock and fell to the ground.

I lay there in terror and despair, my last hope gone. I
would never get out. I would die the most dreadful of deaths.
I tried to speak aloud but no sound came. I could scarcely   *25*
breathe.

Then I noticed a new horror. My lamp had broken when I
fell and was gradually going out. I watched its glow fading.
Shadows passed along the walls. I did not dare shut my eyes
for an instant. The precious light was going, going . . . Final-   *30*
ly it went out altogether and I was in total darkness.

A terrible cry burst from my lips. No light! I was blind! I
stood up, with my arms stretched out in front of me, trying
to feel my way. I started to rush downwards, downwards all
the time, crying, shouting, hurting myself on the sharp rocks,   *35*
falling, getting up again, trying to drink the blood that was
running down my face.

I shall never know where I ran. After several hours, I fell to the ground and fainted.

I hear voices

When I became conscious again, my face was wet with tears. I had no way of knowing how long I had been uncons-
5   cious. No man had ever been so alone.

I was covered with blood from my fall. I did not want to think any more. In pain, wishing I were already dead, I rolled across the floor to the opposite wall.

Then I heard a loud noise like thunder, gradually fading
10 away. Where could it have come from? An underground ex-plosion, perhaps.

I listened, in case it happened again. Quarter of an hour passed in complete silence.

Suddenly my ear, which happened to be against the wall,
15 heard words. They were far away but they were words.

'I'm imagining it!' I thought nervously.

But no. Listening again, I definitely heard voices. I was too weak to understand what was said. But someone was speaking. I was sure of that.

20 For a moment I was afraid that the words might be my own, brought back by an echo. Perhaps I had cried out without knowing. I closed my lips tightly and put my ear against the wall again.

'Yes, someone is speaking.'

25 Even when I dragged myself a few feet farther along the wall, I could hear it. Then I heard a sad voice repeat the word 'lost'.

Who was speaking? Clearly, it was either my uncle or Hans. And if I could hear them, they could hear me.

30 'Help!' I cried as loudly as I could. 'Help!'

I listened for some reply from the darkness, for a shout or even a sigh. None came. Perhaps my voice was too weak to reach my companions.

'It must be them,' I said to myself. 'What other men could
35 be seventy-five miles underground?'

I listened again. Moving my ear around the wall, I found a place where the voices seemed loudest. The word 'lost' reached me again, followed by the same sound like thunder. Then I clearly heard my name. It *was* my uncle, talking to the guide! 5

Suddenly I understood. The sounds weren't coming *through* the wall – they couldn't, it was solid granite – but the sounds were coming *along* the wall.

I talk to my uncle

But I had to hurry, in case my uncle moved away from the wall. I put my mouth against the wall and, as clearly as pos- 10 sible, said, 'Uncle Lidenbrock!'

A few seconds passed which seemed like centuries. At last these words reached me: 'Axel! Axel! Is that you?'

'Yes, yes!' I replied.

'Where are you?' 15

'Lost, in absolute darkness.'

'But your lamp?'

'Gone out.'

'And the stream?'

'Disappeared.' 20

'Axel, my poor boy, cheer up!'

'I'm exhausted. You talk.'

'Have courage,' my uncle continued. 'We've been up and down the passage looking for you, in vain. Oh, I've shed tears for you, my boy. Finally, we came back down the Hansbach, 25 firing our guns. Our hands still cannot touch but don't despair, Axel. At least we can now hear each other.'

Already, faint hope had returned to me. I put my lips close to the wall.

'Uncle!' I said. 30

'Yes, my boy,' came the reply a few seconds later.

'We must know how far apart we are. You have your chromometer?'

'Yes.'

'Then say my name, noticing the exact second at which 35

you speak. As soon as I hear it, I'll repeat my name and you must notice the second at which my reply reaches you.'

'Right. Are you ready?'

'Yes.'

5   'I'm going to say your name now.'

As soon as I heard 'Axel', I replied 'Axel'. Then I waited.

'Forty seconds,' said my uncle. 'There were forty seconds between the time I said 'Axel' and the time I heard you say it. So sound takes twenty seconds to travel between us. At

10   1,020 feet a second, that makes 20,400 feet or just under four miles.'

'Four miles!' I muttered. 'Should I go up or down?'

'Down, and I'll tell you why. We are in a huge cave with many passages leading into it. The one you are in is sure

15   to lead here because all the cracks and gaps seem to start from this place. So get up and start off. Drag yourself along if you have to. Slide down the steep slopes and our arms will be ready to welcome you at the end. Come, my boy, come!'

His words encouraged me.

20   'I'm leaving now, Uncle,' I cried. 'We shan't be able to talk once I've left here, so goodbye!'

'Goodbye, Axel, goodbye!'

Those were the last words I heard. Our amazing conversation, conducted through the earth over a distance of nearly

25   four miles, ended on this note of hope. I realized that, as my uncle's voice had reached me, nothing could be between us. If I followed the sound and if my strength did not fail, I would reach him. I got up, dragging myself along. The slope was quite steep and I let myself slide. I went faster and faster.

30   I no longer had the strength to stop myself. The ground disappeared under my feet. I was falling vertically. My head hit a rock and I lost consciousness.

Saved

When I became conscious again, I was stretched on blankets in half-darkness. My uncle held my hand at my first sigh.

35   When I opened my eyes, he gave a cry of joy.

'He's alive! He's alive!'

'Yes,' I said weakly.

'My dear boy,' said my uncle, taking me in his arms, 'you are saved!'

I was overcome by his words and actions. Such tenderness from the Professor was rare.   5

Then Hans came up and I think there was joy in his eyes, too, when he saw my uncle holding my hand.

'Good day,' he said.

'Good day, Hans, good day,' I whispered. 'Now tell me where we are, Uncle.'   10

'Tomorrow, Axel, tomorrow. Today you are too weak.'

'But at least tell me what time it is, and what day.'

'It's eleven o'clock at night on Sunday, August 9. Now I forbid you to ask more questions until the 10th.'

So I had been alone for three days! I was indeed very weak   15
and I let myself go to sleep again thinking about it.

Next morning when I woke up, I looked around. My bed, made up of all our blankets, was in a delightful cave dotted with stalactites and carpeted with fine sand. No lamps were burning but there was light coming in through a narrow open-   20
ing. I could also hear a mysterious noise like waves on a shore, and then a sound like the wind.

Was I dreaming? Or had my brain been cracked in my fall?

'No, that really is daylight,' I thought, 'slipping in between the rocks. That really is the noise of waves. That is the   25
whistling of the wind. Have we returned to the surface then? Has my uncle given up the expedition or has he finished it successfully?'

The Professor appeared.

'Good morning, Axel,' he said happily. 'Hans and I watched   30
over you all night. You slept well so you must be feeling better.'

'I certainly am,' I said. 'I'll prove it by the speed with which I'll eat any breakfast you give me.'

'Oh, you shall have something to eat, my boy. The fever   35
has left you and, thanks to Hans, your wounds have healed surprisingly fast.'

My uncle prepared some food for me. I ate eagerly while he talked and answered my questions. I learned that my fall had brought me in a torrent of stones right into my uncle's arms!

5   'It's amazing that you weren't killed,' he told me. 'Now don't get separated from us again. Next time it might be for ever.'

Next time? Then the expedition wasn't over? My eyes opened wide.

10   'What's the matter, Axel?' he asked immediately.

'I want to ask something. You say that I'm all right.'

'Yes.'

'And none of my bones is broken.'

'Not one.'

15   'And my head?'

'Your head is fine.'

'Well, I'm afraid that my brain is not.'

'Your brain?'

'Yes. We haven't returned to the surface, have we?'

20   'No, certainly not.'

'Then I must be mad. I can see daylight, and I can hear the wind and the sea.'

'Oh, is that all?'

'Won't you explain?'

25   'I can't explain, but you shall see with your own eyes.'

'Then let's go out!' I cried, sitting up.

'No, Axel. The open air might be bad for you.'

'The open air?'

'Yes, the wind is rather strong.'

30   'But I feel perfectly well.'

'Have a little patience, my boy. Our voyage may be a long one.'

'Voyage?'

'Yes. Rest today and tomorrow, we'll set sail.'

35   'Set sail?'

Was there a river or a lake out there? Was a ship waiting for us, anchored in some underground harbour? My curiosity was so violent that my uncle decided it would do me more harm than the satisfaction of it. He agreed to let me go outside.

I dressed quickly, wrapped one of the blankets around me and left the cave.   5

13 An Underground Sea

At first, I saw nothing. My eyes were not used to the light now and they closed immediately. When I was able to open them again, I was more surprised than delighted.

'The sea!' I cried.

5 'The Lidenbrock Sea,' said my uncle. 'I found it so I have a right to call it by my name!'

Water, the beginning of a lake or an ocean, stretched away out of sight. There was a sloping beach of fine golden sand, covered with small shells; and waves echoed strangely as they
10 broke on it. A wind blew some of the water in my face. Behind the beach, a line of cliffs curved up to great heights.

It was a real sea but empty and wild in appearance.

And the light that showed it to me was neither warm and brilliant like that of the sun, nor cold and pale like that of
15 the moon. It was a strong, cool, white light that was clearly electric.

Over my head, instead of a sky shining with stars, there were huge clouds. The effect was sad. Above those clouds, I knew, there was a granite roof.

20 We were indeed in a cavern, although the word gives no idea of the size. The shore, like the water, stretched out of sight and the clouds, I estimated, were 12,000 feet high.

I did not know what theory could explain such a place. No cave known to man compared with this one with its cloudy
25 sky, its electric light and huge sea. I looked at it in silence. New words were needed for such sights and I could not produce them. I looked, I thought, I admired — with amazement mixed with fear.

But my uncle had stopped being amazed at such wonders.
30 'Do you feel strong enough to walk about a little?' he asked me.

'Yes,' I replied. It was wonderful to breathe that wet, salty air after forty days below ground.

'Then hold my arm, and let us go along the shore.'

On the left, steep rocks were piled on top of each other. Water poured down their sides. Streams flowed gently into the sea and among them I recognized our faithful Hansbach. 5

'We shall miss it in the future,' I said with a sigh.

'Nonsense!' said the Professor ungratefully. 'What does it matter which stream is with us?'

Five hundred yards away, a strange forest appeared. Its 10 trees looked like open umbrellas and they moved not at all with the wind, as if they were made of stone.

I walked faster, anxious to find out what trees they were. When we arrived under their shade, my surprise turned to admiration. 15

'It's just a forest of mushrooms,' said my uncle.

He was right but what mushrooms! I knew there were mushrooms that grew to eight or nine feet but these were white mushrooms thirty or forty feet high, with heads just as big across. And there were thousands of them, crowded 20 so tightly that no light could get between.

I wanted to go further. For half an hour we wandered among those cold, damp shadows and then returned to the shore.

Further on, many other trees with no colour in their leaves 25 stood in groups: the ordinary undergrowth of earth grown to giant size.

'Magnificent, splendid!' cried my uncle. 'All the vegetation of the Secondary Period. Here are our humble garden plants which were trees in the early days of the world. Look, 30 Axel, and admire it all! And look at the bones you are walking on, too.'

'Bones?' I exclaimed. 'Yes, yes! These are the bones of huge prehistoric* animals.'

I picked one up. 35

'Here is the lower jaw of one,' I said, 'and over there is the

*prehistoric, from the time before written history.

leg bone of another. Animals have lived on the shores of this underground sea, in the shade of these giant plants. I can even see some complete skeletons*.'

I had a thought. Some of the monsters might still be alive, wandering in the cold forests or behind the steep rocks. I   5
looked carefully around me in some alarm but I could see nothing.

We were the only living creatures in this underground world. When the wind dropped, the silence was deeper than that of the desert. I tried to look beyond the horizon*. Where   10
did the sea end? Where did it lead? Could we ever hope to cross it?

My uncle did not doubt that we could. I was half hopeful, half frightened.

After another hour, we returned along the beach to the   15
cave, where I fell into a deep sleep.

The raft

I awoke next day completely cured. I swam in the sea for a few minutes, thinking it would do me good, and came back   20
hungry for breakfast.

Hans was the cook and as he now had both fire and water, could do more interesting dishes than usual. He even served coffee. Never had that drink tasted so delicious!

'Now,' said my uncle, 'the tide is rising and we must study   25
it.'

'The tide?' I exclaimed.

'Yes, of course.'

'You mean that the influence of the moon and sun extends down here?'   30

'Why not?'

At that moment we were walking on the sandy beach and, yes, the waves were gradually moving up the shore.

'You are right!' I cried. 'I can scarcely believe my eyes. I should never have thought that, inside the earth's crust,   35
there was a real ocean with tides, winds and storms.'

*skeleton, bone structure of an animal.
*horizon, line at which the earth or sea and sky seem to meet.

'Why not?' said my uncle again. 'Is there any scientific reason against it?'

'None that I know — if we abandon the theory of central heat.'

5   'Then Humphry Davy is right?'

'Clearly. So there may be other seas and continents like this one. And they may contain fish! Let's make some lines and hooks!'

'We will, Axel. We must discover all we can about these
10 new regions.'

'But where exactly are we, Uncle? I haven't asked you that yet.'

'Horizontally, we are 875 miles from Iceland.'

'As far as that? Does the compass still show our direction
15 as south-east?'

'Yes.'

'And how far down are we?'

'Eighty-eight miles.'

'So,' I said, 'the snow-covered mountains of Scotland are
20 above us?'

'Yes,' laughed the Professor. 'It's rather a heavy weight to support but the ceiling is solid. It's built of the best material!'

'Oh, I'm not afraid of the roof falling in,' I said. 'But now, Uncle, what are your plans?'

25 'We shall continue our journey downwards, as everything has been so successful so far.'

'But how can we get below all this water?'

'I'm not going to dive in head first! I'm sure we shall find new openings on the opposite shore.'

30 'And how far do you think that is?'

'Between 70 and 100 miles.'

'Ah!' I said, thinking to myself that this estimate could be quite wrong.

'So we mustn't waste time, we must set sail tomorrow.'

35 I looked around for the boat which would carry us.

'So we must set sail,' I said. 'All right, but where's the boat?'

'It won't be a boat, my boy. It will be a good, solid raft*.'

'A raft?' I cried. 'But a raft is as hard to build as a boat and I don't see . . . '

'You don't see, Axel, but if you listened you might hear.'

'Hear?'   5

'Yes, hear some hammering. Hans is already building our raft. Come and see.'

After walking for quarter of an hour, we found Hans at work in a small natural harbour behind a cliff. To my surprise, a half-finished raft was lying on the sand. It was made   10
of beams of a strange kind of wood and there was a lot more wood like it lying all around.

'What wood is this, Uncle?'

'It's fossil wood, boy, wood that has been turned to mineral by the action of the sea-water.'   15

'But then surely it must be as hard as stone and too heavy to float?'

'Not the pieces that are only partly fossilised. Look,' added my uncle, throwing one such piece into the water.

It disappeared from sight. Then it rose again to the surface   20
and floated on the waves.

'Amazing!' I cried.

Next evening, the raft was finished. It was ten feet long and five feet wide. Its beams were bound with strong ropes to form a solid deck. Its mast* was two sticks tied together,   25
its sail was one of our blankets. We pushed it into the water and it floated peacefully on the Lidenbrock Sea.

*raft, a flat wooden boat.
*mast, tall piece of wood which supports sails.

14 We Set Sail

On August 13 we awoke early, eager to travel this new and easy way.

Everything was loaded on board: food, instruments, tools, fire-arms, a large supply of fresh water. At six o'clock, the Professor ordered us on board, too.

Hans was steering. I let go of the rope that held us to the shore and we moved out.

As we were leaving the little harbour, my uncle suggested we should give it a name, too.

'Mary,' I suggested. 'Port Mary would look very nice on your map.'

'Port Mary it shall be,' agreed my uncle.

The wind was blowing from the north-west. We sailed before it at great speed.

'If we go on at this rate,' said my uncle after an hour, 'we shall travel at least seventy-five miles in twenty-four hours, and it won't be long before we reach the other shore.'

I did not reply but went and sat forward, watching. Soon we were completely out of sight of land.

At about midday, huge pieces of seaweed came floating past. I knew that seaweed could be big enough to stop a ship but none, surely, could be as big as that seaweed on the Lidenbrock Sea. There were pieces 4,000 feet long! What natural force could produce such plants?

Evening came but it did not get dark. The light over this sea was constant. After supper, I stretched out by the mast and fell into a pleasant sleep.

Next day, as my uncle had instructed, I started to keep a diary of our strange voyage. Here are the notes I made:

Friday, August 14. Steady NW wind. Raft sailing fast and straight. Coast seventy-five miles away. Nothing on the horizon. Same constant light. Weather fine. Temperature 32°C.

At midday, Hans fastened a hook and bit of meat on the

end of a line and threw it over the side. For two hours he
caught nothing. We began to think the waters were uninha-
bited. Then the line tightened and Hans pulled in a struggling
fish.

We examined the creature carefully. It was like fish we   5
knew, and yet different. It had, for example, no teeth or tail.

The Professor decided it belonged to an extinct family of
fish known to Man only as fossils.

'What!' I cried. 'You mean we've caught an "extinct" fish
alive?'   10

'Yes,' replied the Professor continuing to look at it, 'and
you'll notice something peculiar about it — something peculiar, so they say, to fish in underground waters.'

'What's that?'

'It's blind.'   15

'Blind?'

'Not only blind. It has no eyes at all.'

I looked at the fish. What my uncle said was true. But as
this creature might be an exception, we threw the line over
the side again. In two hours we caught many fish belonging   20
to 'extinct' families. None of them had eyes.

I looked up in the air. As there were extinct fish around,
why should there not also be extinct birds, feeding on them?

My imagination carried me away and I had a prehistoric
day-dream: first of great animals, then of enormous birds,   25
then of the reptiles* that came before them and of the fish
before *them*.

Farther and farther back I dreamed: of the time before
animals, when plants were the only things that lived in the
great heat; and of the time before plants, when there was no 30
rock but the earth was all gas, white-hot and as big and bright
as the sun.

What a dream! As if in a fever, I wrote down every strange
detail. I forgot everything else — the Professor, the guide, the
raft.   35

'What's the matter?' asked my uncle.

I stared at him without seeing him.

'Be careful, Axel, or you'll fall in.'

*reptile, cold-blooded animal that lays eggs, e.g. snake.

I felt Hans seize me. If he hadn't, I might have thrown myself into the sea.

'Has he gone mad?' cried the Professor.

'What is it?' I said at last.

5   'Are you ill?'

'No, no, I was dreaming. It's over now . . . Is everything all right?'

'Yes, there's a good wind and a fine sea. We should see land soon.'

10   I stood and looked at the horizon. There was still nothing between water and clouds.

Saturday, August 15. No land in sight.

My uncle was in a bad temper. Now that I had recovered, his old impatience had returned.

15   'You seem anxious, Uncle,' I said, seeing him study the horizon through his telescope again and again.

'Anxious? Not at all!'

'Impatient, then.'

'Yes, for a good reason.'

20   'But we are moving very fast.'

'What use is that? This sea is too big!'

I remembered that the Professor had estimated his Lidenbrock Sea was about seventy-five miles across. We had sailed three times that far but there was still no sign of the south

25   shore.

'We aren't going *down*!' the Professor continued. 'It's a waste of time. I didn't come on this trip just to sail on a pond!'

He called this journey a trip, this sea a pond!

30   'But,' I said, 'as we're following the route taken by Saknussemm . . . '

'Well, *are we*?' said my uncle. 'Did Saknussemm come to this sea? Did he cross it? Did that stream lead us to the right place?'

35   'Anyhow, the views are magnificent and . . . '

'I don't care about views! I've decided to do something and I'm going to do it. So don't talk to me about magnificent views.'

I left the Professor alone with his impatience. At six in the evening Hans asked for his wages and the money was counted out.

Sunday, August 16. Nothing new. The same weather. The same electric light. A slightly fresher wind. This sea seems to go on for ever. It must be as big as the Mediterranean or even the Atlantic.

My uncle tied one of our heaviest axes to the end of a rope which he let down 1,200 feet. No bottom. It was difficult to pull the axe up again.

When it was back on board, Hans showed me some deep marks in it. I looked at him.

'Teeth,' he said, opening and shutting his mouth several times to help me understand.

'Teeth!' I said in amazement, looking more closely. Yes, those were definitely the marks of teeth on metal. The jaws that contained them must be powerful indeed. Did they belong to some prehistoric monster that lived deep beneath the surface? A monster more terrible than the shark or whale? Was my day-dream going to come true? I could not forgot the idea.

Monday, August 17. All day I thought of those teeth-marks and the sort of reptile that might have made them. Was I going to meet a prehistoric monster? I watched the sea in terror. Professor Lidenbrock seemed to have had the same idea, if not the same fear for, after examining the axe, he kept looking closely at the ocean.

'Why did he let that axe down?' I said to myself. 'It has disturbed some creature and we may be attacked.'

I looked at our guns to make sure they would work.

Already the water is moving differently. Danger is near. We must keep watch.

Tuesday, August 18. Evening came, although, with this constant light, we only knew because we felt tired. Hans was steering and, during his watch, I fell asleep.

Two hours later, I was woken up violently. The raft had been lifted above the water and thrown a hundred feet or more.

'What's the matter?' cried my uncle. 'Have we hit land?'

Hans pointed to a dark shape rising and falling a quarter of a mile away.

'It's a giant porpoise*!' I cried.

'Yes,' said my uncle, 'and over there is a giant sea-lizard*.'

5   'And farther on a huge crocodile*! Look at its rows of teeth! Oh, it's disappearing.'

'A whale! A whale!' cried the Professor. 'Look at the water it's spouting!'

We stood there looking in surprise and horror at this as-
10   sembly of sea-monsters. The smallest of them could have broken our raft with one bite of its jaws. Hans wanted to turn around but in the other direction he saw creatures just as frightening – a turtle* forty feet long and a serpent* thirty feet long, darting its enormous head this way and that
15   above the waves.

Escape was impossible. The reptiles came closer and closer to the raft. I picked up my rifle but what effect could a bullet have on such creatures?

We were dumb with fright. They came still closer, the cro-
20   codile and the serpent. The rest had disappeared. I got ready to fire but Hans stopped me. The two monsters passed within 100 yards of the raft – and threw themselves at each other without noticing us.

The battle began 200 yards away. We could see the two
25   monsters gripping each other. But then it seemed to me that the other animals had come back and joined in. I pointed them all out to the Icelander but he shook his head.

'Two,' he said.

'He's right,' said my uncle, who had the telescope.

30   'He can't be!' I protested.

'Yes, he is. The first of those monsters has the nose of a porpoise, the head of a lizard and the teeth of a crocodile. It's the most fearful of prehistoric reptiles, the ichthyosaurus!'

35   'And the other?'

'The other is the enemy of the first – a serpent with a

*_porpoise_, large fish.
*_sea-lizard, crocodile, turtle, serpent_, reptiles that live in water.

turtle's shell, the plesiosaurus!'

Hans had been right. Only two monsters were disturbing the surface of the sea — an ichthyosaurus at least a hundred feet long with eyes as big as a man's head, and a plesiosaurus with a neck that rose thirty feet above the water.   5

These two attacked each other with an anger impossible to describe. They made mountainous waves that rolled as far as the raft and nearly turned us over. They made a terrible noise as they fought. They were so close we could not see where one monster began and the other ended.   10

One hour, two hours passed. The fight in all its violence continued. We stood without moving, ready to shoot.

Suddenly both monsters disappeared beneath the water.

Was the fight going to finish in the depths of the sea?

Several minutes passed. Then an enormous head shot out of the water, the head of the plesiosaur. The monster was dying. I could no longer see its shell but its long neck was rising and falling. The water flew all around and almost blinded us. But soon the movements became less violent and the body of the serpent lay stretched out on the calm waves.

Wednesday, August 19. Luckily the wind is blowing hard and we have been able to get quickly away from the scene of the battle. Hans is still steering. My uncle has returned to his impatient examination of the horizon.

Thursday, August 20. Wind NNE. Temperature high. Speed about nine knots*. At about midday, we heard a continuous roaring noise in the distance.

Hans climbed to the top of the mast but could see nothing.

Three hours passed. The roar seemed to be that of a waterfall. I said so to my uncle, who shook his head. There was definitely *something* very noisy out there, quite a few miles away. Was it in the sky or the sea? Both looked calm.

About four o'clock, Hans climbed the mast again. His eyes looked to the horizon and stopped at a certain point.

'He has seen something,' said my uncle.

'Yes, I believe he has.'

Hans came down and pointed to the south.

'Over there,' he said.

My uncle seized his telescope. 'Yes, yes!' he cried.

'What can you see?'

'A huge column of water rising above the waves.'

'Another sea-monster?'

'Perhaps.'

'Then let us steer more to the west. We know how dangerous these monsters are.'

'Straight ahead,' replied my uncle.

I turned to Hans but he steered on.

The nearer we got to the column, the taller it seemed. What creature could take in so much water and shoot it out for so long without stopping?

knot, a sea mile per hour.

At eight o'clock in the evening, we were less than five miles from the monster. Its huge dark body lay in the sea without moving. It seemed to me to be over a mile long. The column of water was being thrown 500 feet in the air and roaring down as rain.   *5*

We were rushing towards a powerful monster that a hundred whales a day could not satisfy! Terror seized me.

Suddenly, Hans pointed at the object and said, 'Island.'

'An island?' I asked doubtfully.

'Why, yes!' replied the Professor, shaking with laughter.   *10*

'But what about that column of water?'

'Geyser,' said Hans.

'Yes, it must be,' agreed my uncle, 'a geyser like those there are in Iceland.'

At first, I refused to believe that I could mistake an island   *15* for a monster. But the proof was in front of me and finally I had to admit it.

The island looked just like a whale with its head sixty feet above the water. Now and then we heard explosions and the enormous column of water shot up to the clouds. The rays of   *20* electric light mixed with it to produce many different colours.

'Let us land,' said the Professor.

Hans skilfully steered the raft up to the island. I jumped on to the rocks and my uncle followed lightly. Hans stayed on board without curiosity.   *25*

The ground was trembling under our feet. It was burning hot. I put the thermometer into the boiling water from which the geyser rose. It said 163°C.

This water was coming from a blazing furnace. There *was* central heat!   *30*

I pointed this out to Professor Lidenbrock.

'We shall see.' That was all he would say.

After naming the island 'Axel', he led the way back to the raft. Hans had put it in order during our absence and now we set sail again.   *35*

We have sailed 675 miles from Port Mary and we are 1,500 miles from Iceland, under England.

15   The Storm

Friday, August 21. Today the magnificent geyser had disappeared: the wind was stronger and had blown us rapidly away from Axel Island.

The weather (if I may use that word) was changing. The air
5 grew heavy, full of electricity. Gradually the clouds in the south swelled up and combined, getting darker all the time.

There was so much electricity around that my hair stood on end. I felt as if my companions would receive a violent shock if they touched me.

10 At ten o'clock in the morning, I had to say it, 'There's bad weather on the way.'

The Professor did not answer. He was in a dreadful temper at the sight of the ocean stretching on and on.

'We're going to have a storm,' I said.

15 There was silence. The wind dropped completely. The raft no longer moved on the sea. Why did we keep up that sail if a storm were coming?

'Let us take in the sail and remove the mast,' I said. 'That would be sensible.'

20 'No, a hundred times no!' shouted my uncle. 'Let the wind seize us! Let the storm carry us away! Providing it carries us on to some shore, I don't care if it smashes the raft to pieces.'

He had scarcely said this when there was a change on the southern horizon. Suddenly, the wind blew with the force of
25 a hurricane*. It became really dark and I could make only a few notes.

The raft rose into the air and leapt forward, throwing my uncle on to the deck. I crawled over to him and found him holding on to a rope, enjoying it. Hans did not move. His
30 long red hair was being blown by the wind over his still face. He looked like prehistoric man himself as he stood there.

*__hurricane,__ a fierce wind.

The raft flew along at a speed I could not calculate. The mast stayed firm, although the sail swelled out like a bubble about to burst.

'The sail! The sail!' I cried, wanting to take it in.

'No!' said my uncle.   5

'No,' repeated Hans, gently shaking his head.

Now the rain roared down. The curtain of cloud was torn apart, the sea boiled. Brilliant lightning mixed with rolls of thunder. Hailstones* struck the metal of our tools and guns, flashing light. Each wave, tipped with flame, looked like a   10
small volcano.

I could hardly see, the light was so bright. I could hardly hear, the thunder was so loud. I had to hang on to the mast, which bent before the storm.

(Here, my notes became very short but they give a better   15
idea of the atmosphere than my memory could.)

Sunday, August 23. Where are we? We have been carried along at enormous speed.

   Last night was dreadful and the storm is still just as strong. The noise is continuous. Our ears are bleeding. It is impossi-   20
ble to talk.

The lightning is flashing all the time.

Where are we going? My uncle is stretched out at one end of the raft.

It is getting hotter. The thermometer says . . . (I can't read   25
what I wrote.)

Monday, August 24. Will this never end? My uncle and I are exhausted. Hans is the same as ever.

The raft is still going south-east. We are over 500 miles from Axel Island.   30

At midday, the storm grew even worse. We had to tie our-selves down. The waves went over our heads.

We had not been able to exchange a word for three days. I think my uncle now said 'We are finished', but I am not sure.

'Let us take in the sail,' I wrote down for him to read. He   35
moved his head in agreement.

*hailstones, pieces of ice falling from the sky.

The fire-ball

At that moment, a ball of fire appeared on the raft itself. The mast and sail disappeared upwards — like a prehistoric bird.

5   Half white, half blue, the fire-ball moved over the deck from one object to another. It went near Hans, who simply stared at it. It went near my uncle, who fell on his knees to avoid it. It came near me, pale and trembling before its heat. It played around one of my feet, which I tried in vain to pull away.

A smell of gas filled the air. Why couldn't I move my foot?
Was it fastened to the deck? I realized that the ball had magnetized all the iron on board: the instruments, tools and guns
were moving about and bumping into each other. The nails of
my boots were stuck to an iron plate in the deck.   5

At last, with a violent effort, I pulled my foot away just as
the ball was going to seize it and carry me away, too.

Suddenly there was a blaze of light. The ball had burst and
we were covered with tongues of fire.

Then everything went dark. I just had time to see my uncle   10
lying on the deck and Hans still steering but 'spitting fire'
under the influence of the electricity.

Tuesday, August 25. I have just returned to consciousness.
The storm is still raging. Forks of lightning are flashing about
like serpents in the sky.   15

We are still at sea and moving at great speed. We have
passed under England, under the Channel, under France,
perhaps under the whole of Europe.

A new noise! Surely it is the sound of the sea breaking
upon rocks . . .   20

16 Saved from the Sea

Here ends my diary, saved from the wreck.

I cannot say what happened when the raft was thrown on to the rocks. I was thrown into the sea and Hans's strong arm saved me from death.

5   The brave Icelander carried me to a beach where I found myself lying next to my uncle. Then he returned to the rocks to save what he could from the wreck.

I could not speak for a whole hour, I was so exhausted. Hans prepared some food which I could not even touch.

10 Painfully, I slept.

Next day, the weather was excellent. I was woken up by the Professor's cheerful voice.

'Well, my boy, have you slept well?'

I almost thought that we were in the house on King's

15 Street, that I was coming down to breakfast on the day I was to marry my poor Mary.

But no. The raft had probably passed under Germany, under my city of Hamburg, under the street where my dear Mary lived. We were separated by only a hundred miles but

20 they were a hundred vertical miles of solid granite!

'Don't you want to tell me how you slept?' asked my uncle.

'I still feel tired,' I replied, 'but you seem very cheerful, Uncle.'

25   'I'm delighted, my boy, delighted! We've arrived.'

'At the end of our expedition?'

'No, but at the end of that sea that seemed to go on for ever. Now we can travel by land again and really go *down.*'

'Uncle, may I ask you a question?'

30   'You may, Axel, you may.'

'What about our return journey?'

'Very simple. We shall either find some new route or go

back the way we came. I don't imagine it will close behind
us.'
'Then we must repair the raft.'
'Of course.'
'But have we enough food to continue?'   5
'Oh, Hans is very clever, I'm sure he saved most of it. Let
us go and see.'

Our possessions are safe
I thought everything must have been destroyed in the   10
wreck, but I was wrong. We found Hans on the shore with
our things neatly arranged around him. My uncle shook his
hand in deep gratitude. While we had been lying on the
beach, the Icelander had risked his life to save our possessions. Our guns had been lost but everything else seemed to   15
be there, including the gun-powder and all the instruments.
'Here is the manometer,' exclaimed the Professor, 'the
most useful instrument of all, the one which will tell me
when we reach the centre. Without it, we might go too far!'
His cheerfulness was frightening.   20
'But where's the compass?' I asked.
'Here on this rock, as well as the chronometer and the
thermometer. Hans is splendid!'
'What about the food?' I asked.
'Let us see,' replied the Professor.   25
The boxes which contained our food were laid out in a
row. Biscuits, salt meat, gin, dried fish . . . We had enough for
another four months.
'Four months!' cried the Professor. 'We have time to get to
the centre and back. With what remains, I shall give a dinner 30
to the other professors at the Johannaeum!'
I ought to have been used to my uncle by now but the
man still amazed me.
'Now,' he said, 'we must fill our bottles with the rain-water
the storm has left in these rocks. And I shall ask Hans to re- 35
pair the raft, although I don't think we shall need it again.'
'Why not?' I cried.

'Just an idea, my boy. I don't think we shall leave by the way we came in.'

He didn't know then how right he was.

'Let's go and have breakfast,' he said.

5   I followed him after he had given instructions to Hans. During the meal – which was one of the best I have ever tasted – I asked the Professor where he thought we were.

'It's certainly difficult to say exactly,' he answered. 'I've not been able to keep a record for the last three days. Still, I
10   can make an estimate.'

'Well, at the island with the geyser . . . '

'Axel Island, my boy, the first island to be discovered under the earth.'

'All right, at Axel Island we had travelled across 675 miles
15   of the Lidenbrock Sea and we were over 1,500 miles from Iceland.'

'Good. Let us start from that point. There were about four days of storm during which we must have travelled at least 200 miles every twenty-four hours.'

20   'That adds up to 800 miles.'

'Yes, and it means the Lidenbrock Sea is about 1,500 miles from shore to shore. Do you realize, Axel, it is as big as the Mediterranean?'

'Yes, especially if we have only crossed the width of it.'

25   'Which is quite possible.'

'What is more,' I said, 'if our calculations are correct, the Mediterranean itself is over our heads!'

'Really?'

'Yes, because we are 2,250 miles from Reykjavik.'

30   'That is a long way my boy, but we can't be sure we are under the Mediterranean unless we are sure our direction did not change during the storm.'

'I'm certain it didn't. The wind seemed to stay the same. I think this shore is south-east of Port Mary.'

35   'Well, we can easily find out by looking at the compass.'

The Professor led the way back to the rock on which Hans had placed the instruments. He was as bright as a young man.

Arriving at the rock, he picked up the compass and looked at the needle. He rubbed his eyes and looked again. Then he turned to me in amazement.

'What's the matter?' I asked.

He told me to look at the instrument. I exclaimed in sur-   5
prise. The north tip of the needle was pointing to what we thought was south! It was pointing towards the land instead of out to sea!

I shook the compass and examined it carefully. It was working perfectly. But wherever I put it, the needle showed   10
this unexpected direction. During the storm, the wind must have changed and brought the raft back to the shore we thought we had left behind.

17 Strange Discoveries

I have never seen a man so surprised at first and so angry afterwards. All those days and dangers to be repeated!

'So air, fire and water combine to stop me, do they?' he shouted. 'Well, they'll see how strong I am! I shan't give up! We shall see whether Man or Nature will win!'

I tried to calm him. 'Listen to me,' I said firmly. 'We can't do the impossible. Nobody can sail against the wind for a thousand miles on a collection of rotten beams with a blanket for a sail and two sticks for a mast. We should be mad to try again . . .'

I was able to continue like this for ten minutes simply because the Professor did not listen to a word I said.

'To the raft!' he cried. That was his only reply. It was no use arguing. His will was harder than granite.

Hans had just finished repairing the raft, as if he had guessed. He put all our things on board. The sky was fairly clear, the wind was blowing steadily from the north-west.

What could I do against the two of them, against such a master and such a servant? I was about to step on board when my uncle stopped me.

'We shan't leave until tomorrow,' he said. 'We must explore this part of the coast now we are here.'

If we had returned to the north shore, you understand, we had not returned to Port Mary. That, we decided, was further west. So it was sensible to inspect this new region.

'Let's start exploring, then,' I said.

Hans stayed with the raft while the Professor and I set off. The space between the sea and the cliffs was very wide at this point. We walked over huge shells in which prehistoric creatures had lived, and over stones that looked like pebbles* rounded by the sea.

*pebble, a stone made round and smooth by the action of water.

'Ah!' I said to myself, 'this explains, to an extent, the existence of the Lidenbrock Sea. Our seas flowed down here through some crack in the earth's surface and now the water has evaporated* a little because of the heat. This is the reason for the clouds and all the electricity.'   5

I was satisfied with this theory. The wonders of Nature can always be explained by physical laws, I thought.

We had walked for about a mile when the ground changed. It became very rough, full of hollows. We were advancing over it with difficulty when suddenly we came upon a plain   10
piled high with bones. Row after row of them stretched away to the horizon. There before us was laid out the entire history of animal life!

We rushed forward, our feet cracking and crushing fossils and bones that museums fight about.   15

I was so surprised I could not say anything. My uncle lifted his long arms towards the clouds, his mouth open, his eyes flashing at the sight of this collection beyond price.

A few minutes later, he seized a bare skull* from the dust.

'Axel! Axel!' he cried in a voice trembling with excitement.   20
'A human head.'

The Professor gives a lecture

To understand my uncle's excitement at finding a skull, you need to know what had happened in Europe just before we left.

In 1863, near Abbeville in France, a human jaw-bone had   25
been found fourteen feet below the ground, together with some stone axes. It was the first human fossil of this sort that had ever been discovered.

Many scientists, including Professor Lidenbrock, believed that it belonged to the Quaternary Period. Others did not be-   30
lieve it was so early. Argument was lively between the two sides.

So you will realize my uncle's joy when he found first a human head and then a complete body of Quaternary Man!

*evaporate, turn to steam.
*skull, the bone structure of the head.

I stood in silent wonder. My uncle, who usually talked so much, was also silent. We lifted the body and leaned it against a rock. It looked back at us out of the hollows of its eyes.

Then my uncle became the Professor once more. Otto 5 Lidenbrock forgot where we were, forgot our journey. He imagined himself back at the Johannaeum, lecturing his students, 'Gentlemen,' he said, 'I have the honour to introduce to you a man of the Quaternary Period. Some scientists have already said they believe such a man existed. Others 10 have said they do not. I know that science has to be careful about discoveries of this sort. I know that science has to be careful about discoveries of this sort. I know that Cuvier and Blu . . .'

Here, my uncle's old trouble started, his inability to say 15 difficult words in public.

'Cuvier and Blu . . .' he repeated.

He could not say it. The words would not come out. The audience at the Johannaeum would have roared with laughter.

'Cuvier and Blumenbach,' he finally managed to say be- 20 tween swear-words, 'have said that such bones are only the bones of animals of the Quaternary Period. But now the whole body stands before you! You can see it, touch it!'

Here the Professor seized the skeleton and held it up.

'You can see that this is a human fossil about six feet tall, 25 of the Caucasian race. Don't smile, gentlemen.'

Nobody was smiling but the Professor was used to seeing faces light up with amusement during his lectures.

'How he got here, I do not know,' he continued. 'Perhaps in the Quaternary Period, parts of the earth's surface slipped 30 down through gaps in the earth's crust. It does not matter. Unless he came here like myself, as a mere tourist, he is Quaternary Man!'

The Professor finished and I clapped loudly. My uncle was quite right and we found more skeletons at every step to 35 prove it.

But then we thought of something alarming. Were these

men already dead when they fell down to the shores of the Lidenbrock Sea? Or had they lived here, in this underground world under this false sky? So far we had seen only fish and sea-monsters. Might human beings also be down here, alive?

A live man

5   We walked on over these piles of bones, driven by our burning curiosity. What other wonders might this cavern contain? What new treasures might we discover for science?

Not caring if we lost our way, the Professor led me further and further from the sea-shore. We pressed forward in silence
10 under the strange electric light that made no shadows.

After another mile, we reached the edge of a huge forest — not a forest of mushrooms like the one at Port Mary but a forest, this time, of the Tertiary Period. Its tall trees and plants were brown and faded-looking from the lack of sun.
15 Its leaves had no colour, its flowers had no scent. It looked almost as if it were made of paper.

My uncle went straight in and, hesitating slightly, I followed him. Since there was so much vegetation, might we not meet more monsters?
20 Suddenly I stopped, holding my uncle back. I thought I saw some enormous animals, not fossils this time but living creatures. Yes, yes! I saw elephants tearing at the trees and eating the branches. So that dream I had of the prehistoric world *was* coming true! And we were unprotected!
25 My uncle looked and looked again.

'Forward!' he said, seizing my arm.

'No!' I cried. 'No! We have no weapons. No human could walk safely among those monsters.'

'No human?' asked my uncle, more quietly. 'You are
30 wrong, Axel. Look. Look over there. I can see a living creature like ourselves, a man!'

I looked unwillingly, but he was right. There, less than a quarter of a mile away, leaning against a tree, was a human being, a shepherd* watching his great flock.

*shepherd, a man who looks after sheep.

But this was not something like the skeletons we had found back there. This was a giant over twelve feet tall with a head as big as a cow's and hair on it like that of a lion. In his hand, he held an enormous branch.

We had not moved since we saw him. But he might see us. *5*
We must run.

'Come on, come on!' I urged my uncle. For the first time in his life, he listened to persuasion.

A quarter of an hour later, we were out of sight of the enemy. *10*

Was it a man we saw? Now, months later, I can't believe that it was. No human being could exist in that underground world. The idea is mad.

However, at the time, we ran dumb with amazement back towards the Lidenbrock Sea. *15*

Luckily we had something else to worry about besides giants. Sometimes, on our way, we saw things that reminded us of Port Mary and made us think we had returned to the north shore. At one point, for instance, I thought I recognized our faithful Hansbach and the cave in which I had returned to life. Then, a few steps further on, everything seemed completely new. *20*

'Clearly,' I said to my uncle, 'the storm has not carried us back to exactly the point from which we set sail. Still, if we follow the coast, we shall probably come to Port Mary.' *25*

'If that is so,' replied my uncle, 'we might as well return to the raft. But are you sure you're right, Axel?'

'It's hard to be sure, Uncle, because all these rocks look so alike. But I think that may be the harbour where Hans built the raft.' *30*

'No, Axel, if it were, we should at least see some sign of our . . . '

We find a knife

'But I *can*!' I shouted, rushing towards something that lay on the sand and picking it up. *35*

I showed my uncle a rusty knife.

'Well, well!' he said. 'So you had this knife when we were here before?'

'No, not I. But you . . . '

'It's not mine. But Icelanders carry weapons of this kind. Hans must have had it and dropped it.'

I shook my head. Hans had never had such a dagger.

'Does it belong to that giant, then?' I cried. 'No, it can't. This blade is steel . . . '

'Calm down, Axel, and think,' interrupted my uncle in his coldest voice. 'This knife is a sixteenth century weapon. It belongs neither to you nor to me, nor to Hans, nor to any other human beings who live down here.'

'You mean . . .?'

'Look at it. We are on the way to a great discovery. That blade has lain on this sand not for a day or a year but for 300 years! And it has been blunted on these rocks!'

'But it didn't get here by itself!' I cried. 'Someone has been here before us!'

'Yes, a man.'

'And that man?'

'That man has carved* his name somewhere with this dagger. He wanted once more to show the way to the centre of the earth. Let us look around.'

Wildly excited, we searched among the rocks, looking into every crack. Presently we reached a place where the sea came up almost to the bottom of the cliffs. Between two rocks, we saw the entrance to a dark tunnel. And there, carved into the rock, appeared two mysterious letters, the initials of the bold traveller.

'A.S.,' cried my uncle. 'Arne Saknussemm! Arne Saknussemm again!'

Fallen rock

At the sight of those two letters, caved 300 years before, I was struck dumb. Yes, after all that had happened to us, I could still be amazed. Not only was the signature of Saknus-

*carve, to cut into rock or wood.

semm on the rock but I was also holding the knife that had
shaped it. Now I *had* to believe in the man and his journey.

Professor Lidenbrock was busy praising Saknussemm's
name.

'Oh, brilliant man!' he cried. 'You have done everything in 5
your power to open to other men the road through the
earth's crust. Even now, after three centuries, they can follow
your footsteps. You have made it possible for other eyes to
see these wonders. Your name, carved here and there, shows
other bold travellers the way, and at the centre of the earth it 10
will be found again. Well, I too shall sign my name on that
last page of granite. As for this cape* seen by you in this sea
first discovered by you, let it be known as Cape Saknussemm!'

When I heard my uncle speaking like this, my own interest
came flooding back. I forgot the dangers of the journey, past 15
and still to come. What another man had done, I would do
too.

'Forward! Forward!' I cried.

I was already rushing towards the tunnel when, surprisingly, the Professor stopped me. 20

'Let us go back to Hans first,' he said, 'and bring the raft
here.'

I had to agree and we started back along the shore.

'Uncle,' I said we walked, 'we have really been very lucky
so far.' 25

'You think so, Axel?'

'Yes, I do. Even that storm was lucky for us. Fine weather
was taking us to the southern shore of the Lidenbrock Sea,
where we should have been lost. The storm brought us back
here, where we found the name of Saknussemm.' 30

'Yes, Axel, I must say it does seem fortunate and I can't
find any explanation for it.'

'What does that matter? Our business is not to explain
facts but to take advantage of them.'

'You may be right, my boy, but . . .' 35

'And now we are going north again, under the northern

*cape, a piece of land which sticks out into the sea.

countries of Europe instead of crawling under the deserts of
Africa or something. That's all I need to know.'

'Yes, Axel, you are right. Everything seems to be working
out well. We are leaving this horizontal sea that could lead us
5   nowhere and now we shall go down, down, down. Do you
realize we're now less than 4,000 miles from the centre?'

'Is that all?' I cried. 'Why, that's nothing. Let's go!'

We were still having this crazy conversation when we got
back to Hans. Everything was ready and we sailed straight for
10   Cape Saknussemm.

At about six in the evening, after three hours' slow sailing,
we arrived. I jumped out on to the sand followed by the
others. I was still just as eager. I even suggested burning the
raft to make retreat impossible. But my uncle refused. I
15   thought him very dull.

'At least,' I said, 'let's start without delay.'

'Yes, my boy. But let us look into the tunnel first to see if
we shall need the ladders.'

The Professor took his lamp and I led the way to the
20   opening twenty yards away. It was about five feet across and
level with the ground so we were able to enter without
difficulty. After about six steps, however, the way was
blocked by a huge rock.

'Oh, no!' I shouted angrily.

25   We looked to right and left, up and down, for a way
through. There was no gap.

Disappointed, I sat down on the ground. My uncle
marched backwards and forwards.

'But what about Saknussemm?' I cried.

30   'Yes,' said my uncle, 'was he stopped by this rock?'

'No, no!' I exclaimed. 'It must have fallen after his return
to the surface. Perhaps it was loosened during a storm like
the one we met. Anyhow, if we don't move it, we are not fit
to reach the centre of the earth.'

35   That was how I spoke! The Professor's soul had passed
straight into me. I forgot the past and scorned the future.
Nothing existed on the surface for me any longer, neither
Hamburg, nor King's Street, nor even poor Mary.

'Well,' said my uncle, 'let us break it with our axes.'

'It's too hard for axes.'

'Then what?'

'Gunpowder, of course. We'll blast it!'

'Hans! To work!' cried my uncle. 5

The Icelander returned to the raft to fetch an axe and the gunpowder.

'We shall get through!' I said in high excitement.

'We shall get through,' repeated my uncle.

By midnight, our preparations were finished. Hans had 10 made a hole in the rock big enough to hold the gunpowder, and a slow match of damp gunpowder packed in a long tube was connected to it from just outside. One spark and . . .

'Tomorrow,' said the Professor. I had to wait another six long hours. 15

18 Down into the Abyss

The next day, Thursday August 27, was a turning-point in
our journey. Even now, I remember it with fear.

At six o'clock we were up. It was time to blast the granite.

I asked for the honour of lighting the fuse*. We estimated
5 that the match would burn for ten minutes before reaching
the gunpowder, so I had plenty of time to light it and run
back to join my companions on the raft.

After a quick breakfast, my uncle and Hans went on board
while I stayed on the shore with a lantern*.

10 'Off you go, my boy,' said the Professor, 'and come
straight back here after you have lit the match.'

'Don't worry,' I replied, 'I shan't stop to play!'

I went to the tunnel entrance, opened the lantern and
picked up the end of the match. The Professor was holding
15 his chronometer.

'Ready?' he called out.

'Yes, I'm ready.'

'Then fire, my boy!'

I held the end of the match in the flame, saw it light up
20 and ran back to the edge of the water.

'Oh board,' said my uncle, 'and let's go!'

Hans pushed the loaded raft about sixty feet out to sea.

It was an exciting moment. The Professor was watching his
chronometer.

25 'Another five minutes,' he said. 'Another four... three...
two... one... Now, you granite mountain, down you go!'

What happened then? I don't think I heard the noise of the
explosion. But the rocks opened like a curtain before my
eyes. A pit opened in the shore itself. The sea turned into one
30 enormous wave on top of which stood our raft.

*fuse, cord which carries a spark to explode powder.
*lantern, lamp which gives light with a flame.

We are carried along

All three of us were thrown flat on our faces. There was total darkness. There seemed to be nothing underneath the raft at all. The roar of the water was too loud for us to speak but I realized what had happened. Behind the rock we had
5 just blown up was — an abyss. And the sea was now pouring into it, carrying us too.

I gave up all hope.

An hour passed, perhaps two hours, I don't know. We held hands to save ourselves from being thrown off the raft.
10 Sometimes it hit the side violently but, as this did not happen too often, I thought that the tunnel must be opening out. This was the way Saknussemm had come all right but, instead of following him by ourselves, we had been silly enough to bring a whole sea with us.
15 We seemed to be going down almost vertically and very, very fast.

Our second battery lamp had been broken in the explosion but suddenly Hans managed to light the lantern. The flame was unsteady but it helped a little in the frightening darkness.
20 The tunnel had indeed opened out. In the dim lantern light, we could not see both sides at once. I estimated that we were travelling between them at something like 80 miles an hour.

My uncle and I looked around in despair, hanging on to
25 what remained of the mast and turning our backs to the rush of air. The hours went by. I discovered that of our instruments, only the compass and chronometer remained. Of our tools, there was only a bit of cord tied around the broken mast. Worst of all, the only food was a piece of salt meat and
30 a few biscuits.

Bravely, I did not tell my uncle this latest horror. I wanted him to stay cool and in control.

At that moment, the lantern went out. We still had a torch but could not keep it lit. Like a child, I closed my eyes to
35 avoid seeing all that darkness.

Down and down we fell. My uncle and Hans held me firmly by the arms and still the raft was carrying all three of us.

Going up

I suppose it was about ten o'clock that night when I *heard*
silence fall. The roar of the water had suddenly stopped.

'We are going up!' my uncle shouted. 'We are, we are going   5
up!'

I stretched out my arm and touched the wall, hurting my
hand. We were rising extremely fast.

'The torch! The torch!' cried the Professor.

With some difficulty, Hans lit it.   10

'I thought so,' said my uncle. 'We are in a passage about 20
feet across. The water has reached the bottom of the abyss
and is now levelling out, rising and taking us with it.'

'Taking us where?'

'I don't know but we must be ready for anything. We are   15
rising at about twelve feet a second, or about eight miles an
hour. At this rate, we shall go a long way.'

'Yes,' I said, 'if we are not crushed by anything in the
passage.'

'Axel,' said the Professor very calmly, 'we may die at any   20
moment but, equally, we may be saved at any moment. Let
us be ready to seize any opportunity.'

'But what shall we do now?'

'Eat to make ourselves strong.'

'Eat?' I repeated. Now he had to be told.   25

'What?' cried my uncle. 'All our food gone?'

'Yes, except one piece of meat. Do you still think we can
be saved?'

He did not reply.

An hour passed. We all began to feel hungry but none of us   30
dared to touch that last bit of food.

Meanwhile, we were still rising fast. And the temperature
was rising, too. At that point, it must have been 40 °C. In
spite of Humphry Davy, Otto Lidenbrock and our experience
so far, I still believed in the theory of central heat. Were we   35

finally coming to a place where the heat reduced rock to liquid?

'If we are neither drowned nor crushed and if we don't die of hunger,' I said to the Professor, 'we may still be burnt 5 alive.'

Again, he did not reply. Another hour passed, during which the temperature rose slightly. At last my uncle spoke, 'If we suddenly get that opportunity to save ourselves, how shall we be able to take it, if we are weak from hunger?'
10 'Then you haven't given up hope?' I cried.

'Certainly not,' the Professor replied in a firm voice. 'No creature with will-power should ever despair.'

What splendid words! The man was extraordinary.

'Then what do you suggest we do?'
15 'Eat all the food that is left. This may be our last meal but at least we shall become men again.'

'Very well. Let us eat,' I agreed.

My uncle divided the meat and biscuits equally into three and gave each of us our share. The Professor ate his with a 20 sort of greedy excitement. I ate without pleasure in spite of my hunger. Hans ate quietly and slowly, calmly enjoying each mouthful. He had found half a bottle of gin and offered it around.

'Very good,' said Hans, drinking.
25 'Excellent,' said my uncle.

A little hope had returned to me. But our last meal was over. It was five in the morning and we were silent again.

I wondered what Hans was thinking. For my part, I thought of the house on King's Street which I should never 30 have left, of poor Mary and dear old Martha.

But my uncle never forgot his work. Torch in hand, he was carefully examining the rocks we were passing, trying to discover from them where we were. In spite of myself, I began to be interested.
35 'Granite,' he said. 'We are still in the Primitive Period. But we are going up, going up, so what next?'

With his hand, he felt the side of the passage and a few

moments later he went on, 'This is gneiss! And this is mica-
schist! Good. We shall soon come to . . . '
   But now the temperature was rising fast. We had to take
off first our jackets, then our waistcoats*.
   'Are we going up into a furnace?' I cried.   5
   'Impossible, impossible!' replied my uncle.
   'All the same,' I said, feeling the side, 'this wall is burning
hot.'
   My hand touched the water too and I quickly removed it.
   'The water is boiling!' I cried.   10
   The Professor shook his head at me angrily.
   Then terror seized me. An idea formed in my mind which I
did not dare put into words. Everything I saw made me more
and more certain that I was right. By the light of the torch, I
saw that the granite wall of the passage was slowly beginning   15
to move. Add to that the heat, the boiling water . . . I decided
to look at the compass.
   It had gone mad!

*_waistcoat_, garment worn under a jacket.

19 Shot out of a Volcano

Yes, the compass had gone mad. The needle was swinging around to every point in turn.

And that wasn't all. There were loud explosions, more and more of them, until the noise was like continuous thunder.

5   I was right. The whole mineral crust was going to burst apart and crush us.

'Uncle, Uncle,' I cried. 'This is the end!'

'What's the matter now?' he replied calmly.

'What's the matter? Look at these shaking walls, this heat,
10 this boiling water, this crazy needle — all the signs of an earthquake*!'

My uncle shook his head gently.

'An earthquake?' he asked.

'Yes!'

15   'My boy, I don't think you're right.'

'What! Don't you recognize the signs?'

'Of an earthquake? No. I am expecting something better than that.'

'What do you mean?'

20   'It's an eruption, Axel.'

'An eruption? You mean you think we are inside an active volcano?'

'I do,' said the Professor with a smile, 'and I'm delighted.'

Delighted? Had my uncle gone crazy, too?

25   'What!' I exclaimed. 'We are caught in the middle of an eruption. We are path of burning lava and boiling water. We are going to be thrown out into the air among rocks and flames. And you say you are delighted!'

'Yes,' replied the Professor, looking at me over the top of
30 his glasses. 'Because it's our only chance of returning to the surface.'

*earthquake, violent movement of the earth.

He was right, of course, absolutely right. And never had he seemed bolder than at that moment when he was calmly weighing the possibility of being caught in an eruption.

We continued to rise. Night came and we were still going up, with the noise around us getting louder all the time.   5

We were in the chimney of a volcano, that was certain. But this time, instead of an extinct one like Sneffels, it was a fully active one. Under the raft was boiling water and under that, a whole lot of lava and rocks which would be scattered in all directions when they were shot out of the crater. We were   10 about to die – yet I started wondering in what part of the world we should be shot out. I was sure it would be somewhere in the north. Before it had gone mad, the compass needle had shown we were going north. From Cape Saknussemm we had been carried north for hundreds of miles. Were   15 we now under Iceland again? Would we be shot out of one of its eight volcanoes?

Towards morning, our ascent became faster. Now I noticed deep tunnels on both sides of us, pouring out steam and flame.   20

'Look, Uncle, look!' I cried, pointing at them. 'What if we choke?'

'We shan't. The chimney is getting wider.'

'And what about the rising water?'

'There's no water now, Axel. It's a sort of lava paste that is   25 carrying us up.'

The liquid column had indeed changed into a sort of boiling paste that was carrying us to the mouth of the crater. By now, the temperature must have been over 70 °C.

The raft stops

At about eight in the morning, something new happened.   30 The ascent suddenly stopped and the raft lay quite still. Was it caught on something? No, the paste column itself had stopped moving.

'Has the eruption finished?' I cried.

'Ah, my boy,' said my uncle, 'you are afraid that it has,   35 aren't you? But don't worry. Before long, we shall start moving again.'

'The Professor watched his chronometer as he spoke. Once again he was proved right. Soon the raft started moving and
5 rose fast for about about two minutes. Then it stopped again.

'Good,' said my uncle. 'Ten minutes from now it will start again. This is a volcano with an intermittent* eruption – which allows us to recover our breath!'

How many times it happened, I cannot say. For a few
10 minutes the raft would shoot upwards with such force that the burning air took my breath away. Then for ten minutes it would stop while we nearly choked with the heat.

I thought how wonderful it would be suddenly to find myself in the snow. I imagined myself rolling on the cold
15 white carpet of the Pole. More than once, as my brain weakened, Hans's arms saved me from being dashed against the side.

During the following hours, I remember only continuous explosions, moving rocks and the raft spinning around. It
20 rocked on waves of lava, it was surrounded by roaring flames. A hurricane seemed to be fanning the underground fires.

For the last time I saw Hans's face in the flames. Then came all the terror of the final explosion. I felt like a man tied to the mouth of a cannon* just as the shot is fired.

Back to the surface
25   When I opened my eyes again, I was lying on a mountain slope. Hans's strong hand held my belt. With his other hand, he was supporting my uncle. I was not seriously hurt, though I was scratched all over.

'Where are we?' asked my uncle, who seemed extremely
30 annoyed at being back on the surface of the earth.

'In Iceland,' I said.

'No,' said Hans.

'What, not in Iceland?' cried the Professor.

*intermittent, not continuous.
*cannon, an enormous gun.

I sat up. After all the surprises of our journey, here was one more. I expected to see a peak covered with snow but uncle, the Icelander and I were lying half-way down a mountain baked by the rays of a very hot sun.

I could not believe my eyes. I wanted Iceland at least, I would accept nothing else. The Professor was the first to speak.

'It certainly doesn't look like Iceland,' he said. 'This is no northern volcano with a cap of snow.'

'All the same . . . '

'Look, Axel, look!'

Above our heads, 500 feet up, there was a volcano erupting every quarter of an hour. Below us, streams of lava stretched for about 800 feet. At the base of the mountain grew olive trees and vines heavy with purple grapes.

I had to admit that this was no land of snow. I looked further and saw that we were on a magic island, set in a lovely sea. To our east was a little harbour with a few houses and strange ships rocking on its blue waves. In the distance were more small islands, more mountains. To the north, a great sheet of water glittered in the sun.

It was beautiful and even more beautiful because it was so unexpected.

'Where are we? Where are we?' I kept asking.

Hans closed his eyes, not caring.

'Wherever we are,' said my uncle, 'it's rather hot and the eruption is still going on. It would be a pity to come safely out of a volcano and then be hit on the head by a piece of rock. Let's go down out of the way. Anyhow, I'm dying of hunger and thirst.'

I could have stayed there for hours but I had to follow my companions. The sides of the volcano were steep but I talked away in my excitement, 'We are in Asia!' I cried. 'We must be on the coast of India or Malaya . . . '

'But what about the compass?' said my uncle.

'Yes, of course, the compass,' I said puzzled. 'According to the compass, we were travelling north all the time.'

'Then was it lying?'

'Lying? No, how could it?'

'Then this is the North Pole?'

'The Pole? No, but . . . '

There was a mystery here and I did not know what to   5
think − except that I was feeling hungry, too.

We discover where we are

Fortunately, after walking for two hours, we reached a
lovely place, full of fruit trees. What a delight it was to bite
off whole bunches of purple grapes and to drink from a
spring of fresh water!   10

While we were thus enjoying ourselves, a small boy in rags
appeared between the trees. Frightened at the sight of three
half-naked, bearded strangers, he tried to run away. Hans
caught him and brought him back to us, kicking and
screaming.   15

'What is the name of this mountain?' my uncle asked him
kindly in German.

The child did not answer.

'Good,' said my uncle, 'we are not in Germany.'

He then asked the same question in English.   20

Still the child did not answer.

'Is the boy dumb!' cried the Professor. Proud of his
knowledge of languages, he repeated the question in French.

The same silence.

'Then let's try Italian,' said my uncle, and asked his ques-   25
tion again.

'Stromboli,' said the shepherd-boy and ran off through the
trees.

Stromboli! We were in the middle of the Mediterranean!

'Stromboli! Stromboli!' I repeated.   30

'Stromboli!' cried my uncle.

Oh, what a journey! What a wonderful journey! We had
gone in by one volcano and come out by another more than
3,000 miles away. We had exchanged Sneffels for Stromboli,
the grey fog of Iceland for the blue skies of Italy!   35

We set off now for the port and on the way I heard my uncle muttering, 'But the compass! The compass! It said north! How can we explain that?'

'Why bother to explain it?' I said.

5   'What! A professor at the Johannaeum unable to explain something! The idea is disgraceful!'

As he spoke, half-naked but putting his glasses firmly on his nose, my uncle became once more the frightening professor of mineralogy.

10   An hour later, we reached the port of San Vicenzo where Hans claimed his thirteenth week's wages. My uncle gave them to him and we both shook his hand.

At that moment, something extraordinary happened. The Icelander began to smile.

20   Home Again

The truth would have frightened them, so we told the Stromboli fishermen that we had been shipwrecked. They were most kind. They gave us food and clothing and, on August 31, a small boat took us to Messina in Sicily.

Here we rested until Friday, September 4 when we sailed   5
on a French boat to Marseilles. Our only worry by this time was that compass. Its strange behaviour bothered me all the way to Hamburg, where we arrived on the evening of September 9.

I shan't try to describe Martha's amazement and Mary's   10
joy at our return.

'Now that you are a hero,' said my little Mary, 'you will never need to leave me again.' She smiled at me through her tears.

In Hamburg, Professor Lidenbrock's return caused great   15
excitement. Thanks to Martha, the whole world knew that he had set off for the centre of the earth. People had refused to believe it and when they saw him again, they still refused to. Gradually, however, as they saw Hans and heard from Iceland, they changed their minds.   20

My uncle then became a great man and I became the nephew of a great man.

Hamburg gave a great dinner in his honour. A public meeting was held at the Johannaeum, at which the Professor told the story of his expedition (leaving out only the mystery   25
of the compass). He gave Saknussemm's parchment to the city and modestly said he was sorry he had not been able to follow the Dane right to the centre of the earth.

He defended his theory of gradual cooling to scientists all over the world. For my part, I could not agree with him here.   30
In spite of what we saw, I believed, and still do believe, in the idea of central heat.

At this point, something very sad happened to both of us. Hans left Hamburg. The man to whom we owed our lives, would not stay any longer as our guest. He wanted to be back in Iceland.

5 'Goodbye,' he said one day and returned to Reykjavik. We shall never forget our eider-hunter and I certainly intend to see him again.

I should add that this *Journey to the Centre of the Earth* became world-famous. It was translated into all languages and
10 eagerly discussed, attacked and defended through the newspapers. My uncle enjoyed fame in his own lifetime.

The compass problem is solved

But one thing spoilt his happiness. He didn't understand the behaviour of the compass and, to a scientist, something unexplained is a constant annoyance.
15 One day about six months after our return, while I was arranging a collection of minerals in the Professor's study, I noticed the famous compass lying in a corner. I cried out in surprise. Professor Lidenbrock came running in.

'What's the matter?' he asked.
20 'The compass!'

'Well?'

'The needle points south instead of north!'

My uncle looked, compared the compass with another and then gave a leap of joy which shook the house. The mystery
25 was solved.

'So,' he exclaimed as soon as he could speak again, 'after our arrival at Cape Saknussemm, the needle of this compass pointed south instead of north?'

'Clearly.'
30 'Then that explains our mistake. But why did it do it?'

'It's all very simple.'

'Explain yourself, my boy.'

'During the storm on the Lidenbrock Sea,' I said, 'that fireball which magnetized all the iron on the raft also reversed
35 the poles of our compass.'

'Ah-ha!!' cried the Professor, bursting into laughter. 'So it was a practical joke that electricity played on us!'

From that day, my uncle was the happiest of scientists. And I was the happiest of men for my pretty Mary took her place in the King's Street house as both wife and niece. Her uncle, of course, was the famous Professor Otto Lidenbrock.

Questions

Chapter 1
1. What sort of man was Professor Lidenbrock?
2. What did he teach at the Johannaeum?
3. Who lived in the house on King's Street?
4. What did the Professor keep in his study?
5. What language was the old book written in?
6. What are Runes?
7. To whom had the book once belonged?
8. What language did the Professor think the puzzle was written in?
9. Why did Axel stop listening when he saw the picture of Mary?

Chapter 2
1. How did Axel discover how to read the puzzle?
2. Why did he try to burn the piece of parchment?
3. How long did the Professor sit in his chair trying to work out the puzzle?
4. Why did Axel finally tell him how to read it?
5. Where did Saknussemm claim to have travelled?
6. Where is Sneffels?
7. Why did the Professor think it would be safe to go down into it?
8. Why did Axel think it would be impossible?

Chapter 3
1. What did Mary think of the idea of going to the centre of the earth?
2. What was happening at the house when Axel and Mary returned?
3. Why was the Professor in a hurry to get to Copenhagen?

Chapter 4
1. How did Professor Lidenbrock and his nephew travel to Copenhagen?
2. Why did the Professor make Axel climb the church spire?
3. Which countries did the ship sail past on the way to Iceland from Denmark?

4. How long was the voyage?
5. At whose house did the two travellers stay in Reykjavik?
6. Why were there no books by Saknussemm in the Reykjavik library?
7. Why did the Professor call the volcano 'Seffel' and 'Fessel' to the schoolmaster?
8. What language could the guide speak?

Chapter 5
1. What did the guide look like?
2. How many packs did they take and what was in them?
3. Why did the Professor decide to take no supply of water?
4. How did Axel and his uncle travel from Reykjavik to Stapi? How did Hans travel?
5. How many rooms did the house at Gardär have? And how many people lived in it?
6. What did the Professor give Hans on Saturday, June 20?
7. Who would carry everything from Stapi to the top of Sneffels?
8. Why was Professor Lidenbrock sure that Sneffels was not about to erupt?

Chapter 6
1. Why would Hans not allow the party to stop at seven in the evening? Where did it sleep the night in the end?
2. What could Axel see from the top of Sneffels?
3. How deep did the crater look?
4. What did Professor Lidenbrock find at the bottom of it?

Chapter 7
1. Why would it be difficult to descend the chimney?
2. How did the Professor solve the problem?
3. Who carried the instruments? Who carried the clothes?
4. How far down the chimney did the three go on that first day?

Chapter 8
1. How many battery lamps did they have?
2. Why did Axel think the tunnel looked magnificent?

3. How hot was it at the entrance to the tunnel on June 29, and how hot was it inside the tunnel by eight that same evening?
4. Which passage did the Professor choose when the tunnel divided?
5. How did Axel know they were going the wrong way?

Chapter 9 1. How much water remained by Friday evening (July 3)?
2. Why did they stop walking at six o'clock on Saturday evening (July 4)?
3. What did Professor Lidenbrock save for his nephew?
4. What did Hans refuse to do?
5. What did the Professor promise his nephew?
6. Why did they believe the western passage was the correct one?
7. Why did the Professor say 'It's all over!'?

Chapter 10 1. Why did the Professor and his nephew follow Hans further down the passage?
2. Why did the guide pick up his axe?
3. Why was the stream named the 'Hansbach'?

Chapter 11 1. How deep into the earth were they by Friday, July 10?
2. And how deep were they by Wednesday, July 15?
3. Where did Axel think they must be?
4. Why did Axel think (on Sunday, July 19) that they could not be forty-eight miles below the surface?
5. And why did he think it would take nearly $5\frac{1}{2}$ years to reach the centre of the earth?

Chapter 12 1. What happened on August 7 when Axel was in front?
2. Why did he now need the Hansbach more than ever?
3. What two disasters happened to Axel when he started looking for the stream?
4. What did Axel hear as he lay by himself?
5. How did the sound reach him?
6. How did Axel and his uncle work out how far apart they were?

7. Where did Axel wake up on Sunday, August 9?
8. Why did he think his brain had been damaged?

Chapter 13
1. What had his uncle called the sea he had found?
2. What sort of light was there outside the grotto?
3. Why did the trees look like umbrellas?
4. In which direction did the compass show they had been travelling?
5. How deep were they now?
6. How would they cross the sea?

Chapter 14
1. What name did Axel suggest for the little harbour?
2. Why did it not get dark at night?
3. What was peculiar about all the fish they caught?
4. What did Axel dream?
5. Why did Professor Lidenbrock keep looking through his telescope?
6. What marks appeared on the axe?
7. How many monsters did they see from the raft?
8. What monster did they see on August 20?
9. How far were they now from Iceland?

Chapter 15
1. Why did Axel's hair stand on end?
2. Why would the Professor not take in the sail?
3. What did the fire-ball do on the raft?

Chapter 16
1. What did Hans save from the wreck?
2. Why did the Professor and his nephew look at the compass?
3. Where did it point?

Chapter 17
1. Why was the Professor so angry?
2. What did he and his nephew find when they started exploring?
3. Why was the Professor now so excited?
4. What did he pretend to do?
5. What did Axel see in the 'Tertiary' forest?
6. What did his uncle point out next?
7. Why did the Professor think the dagger had lain on the beach for 300 years?

8. Why did Axel say the storm had been lucky for them?
9. Why did he forget all about Germany at this point?

Chapter 18   1. Why did Hans push the raft sixty feet out to sea?
2. What happened when the slow match reached the gun-powder?
3. How much food was left on the raft after it did?
4. What was rising besides the raft?
5. Why did the Professor suggest they ate the remaining food?
6. Why did he examine the rocks they were passing in the shaft?

Chapter 19   1. What did Axel think was going to happen?
2. How did the Professor correct him?
3. Why did the raft keep stopping?
4. How did they know they had not landed in the north?
5. Why did the Professor want to go further down the mountain?
6. How did he discover where they were?

Chapter 20   1. How long did it take the three of them to get back to Hamburg?
2. What did the Professor give to the city?
3. Why did he leap for joy six months later?

Oxford Progressive English Readers

Introductory Grade

Vocabulary restricted to 1400 headwords
Illustrated in full colour

The Call of the Wild and Other Stories	Jack London
Emma	Jane Austen
Jungle Book Stories	Rudyard Kipling
Life Without Katy and Seven Other Stories	O. Henry
Little Women	Louisa M. Alcott
The Lost Umbrella of Kim Chu	Eleanor Estes
Stories from Vanity Fair	W.M. Thackeray
Tales from the Arabian Nights	Retold by Rosemary Border
Treasure Island	R.L. Stevenson

Grade 1

Vocabulary restricted to 2100 headwords
Illustrated in full colour

The Adventures of Sherlock Holmes	Sir Arthur Conan Doyle
Alice's Adventures in Wonderland	Lewis Carroll
A Christmas Carol	Charles Dickens
The Dagger and Wings and Other Father Brown Stories	G.K. Chesterton
The Flying Heads and Other Strange Stories	Retold by C. Nancarrow
The Golden Touch and Other Stories	Retold by R. Border
Great Expectations	Charles Dickens
Gulliver's Travels	Jonathan Swift
Hijacked!	J.M. Marks
Jane Eyre	Charlotte Brontë
Lord Jim	Joseph Conrad
Oliver Twist	Charles Dickens
The Stone Junk	Retold by D.H. Howe
Stories of Shakespeare's Plays 1	Retold by N. Kates
Tales from Tolstoy	Retold by R.D. Binfield
The Talking Tree and Other Stories	David McRobbie
The Treasure of the Sierra Madre	B. Traven
True Grit	Charles Portis

Grade 2

Vocabulary restricted to 3100 headwords
Illustrated in colour

The Adventures of Tom Sawyer	Mark Twain
Alice's Adventures Through the Looking Glass	Lewis Carroll
Around the World in Eighty Days	Jules Verne
Border Kidnap	J.M. Marks
David Copperfield	Charles Dickens
Five Tales	Oscar Wilde
Fog and Other Stories	Bill Lowe
Further Adventures of Sherlock Holmes	Sir Arthur Conan Doyle

Grade 2 (cont.)

The Hound of the Baskervilles	Sir Arthur Conan Doyle
The Missing Scientist	S.F. Stevens
The Red Badge of Courage	Stephen Crane
Robinson Crusoe	Daniel Defoe
Seven Chinese Stories	T.J. Sheridan
Stories of Shakespeare's Plays 2	Retold by Wyatt & Fullerton
A Tale of Two Cities	Charles Dickens
Tales of Crime and Detection	Retold by G.F. Wear
Two Boxes of Gold and Other Stories	Charles Dickens

Grade 3

Vocabulary restricted to 3700 headwords
Illustrated in colour

Battle of Wits at Crimson Cliff	Retold by Benjamin Chia
Dr Jekyll and Mr Hyde and Other Stories	R.L. Stevenson
From Russia, with Love	Ian Fleming
The Gifts and Other Stories	O. Henry & Others
The Good Earth	Pearl S. Buck
Journey to the Centre of the Earth	Jules Verne
Kidnapped	R.L. Stevenson
King Solomon's Mines	H. Rider Haggard
Lady Precious Stream	S.I. Hsiung
The Light of Day	Eric Ambler
Moonraker	Ian Fleming
The Moonstone	Wilkie Collins
A Night of Terror and Other Strange Tales	Guy De Maupassant
Seven Stories	H.G. Wells
Stories of Shakespeare's Plays 3	Retold by H.G. Wyatt
Tales of Mystery and Imagination	Edgar Allan Poe
20,000 Leagues Under the Sea	Jules Verne
The War of the Worlds	H.G. Wells
The Woman in White	Wilkie Collins
Wuthering Heights	Emily Brontë
You Only Live Twice	Ian Fleming

Grade 4

Vocabulary within a 5000 headwords range
Illustrated in black and white

The Diamond as Big as the Ritz and Other Stories	F. Scott Fitzgerald
Dragon Seed	Pearl S. Buck
Frankenstein	Mary Shelley
The Mayor of Casterbridge	Thomas Hardy
Pride and Prejudice	Jane Austen
The Stalled Ox and Other Stories	Saki
The Thimble and Other Stories	D.H. Lawrence